Introduction to
Computer
Applications
A Hands-On Approach

Apple Version

This text introduces the three major applications packages
available today: word processors, data base managers, and
spreadsheets. To use this book, you will need AppleWorks,
an integrated applications software program, published by
Apple Computer, Inc., and a student activities disk
available from McGraw-Hill.

About the Authors

Arthur Luehrmann and Herbert Peckham are pioneers in the field of computer education. They have worked extensively with educators at all levels to develop methods for teaching about computers. They are the authors of many books and articles on programming, the computer curriculum, and computers. Each was trained as a physicist and has taught physics. Together with Martha Ramírez, they formed the partnership Computer Literacy to develop educational materials for a national computer curriculum.

Arthur Luehrmann did his undergraduate and graduate work at the University of Chicago. Dr. Luehrmann coined the phrase "computer literacy" in 1972, and he has worked to make the concept of computer literacy an integral part of American education. Formerly, he was associate director of the Lawrence Hall of Science at the University of California, Berkeley. He now devotes full time to writing and speaking about computer literacy.

Herbert Peckham graduated from the United States Military Academy and pursued further graduate studies. He has taught physics, computer science, and mathematics at Gavilan College. He is a widely published author of educational materials for use with computers.

Introduction to
Computer
Applications
A Hands-On Approach

Apple Version

Arthur Luehrmann

Herbert Peckham

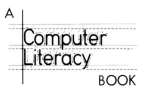

A
Computer
Literacy
BOOK

McGraw-Hill Book Company

New York   St. Louis   San Francisco   Auckland   Bogotá   Guatemala   Hamburg
Johannesburg   Lisbon   London   Madrid   Mexico   Montreal   New Delhi   Panama
Paris   San Juan   São Paulo   Singapore   Sydney   Tokyo   Toronto

Editor: Nola J. Hague

Editorial Assistants: William Farancz, Rudy Rodriguez, John Shane, Ray Simon

Editing and Styling Management: Mary Ann Jones

Editing: Harriet Serenkin

Design and Production Management: Suzanne LanFranchi

Production: Judith Tisdale

Cover Design: A Good Thing, Inc.

PHOTO CREDITS

1: (opposite) F.B. Grunzweig/Photo Researchers
64: Richard Wood/Taurus Photos
100: F.B. Grunzweig/Photo Researchers

This book was set in 11 point Century Schoolbook by York Graphic Services, Inc.

ISBN 0-07-049243-3

1 2 3 4 5 6 7 8 9 10 DOCDOC 94 93 92 91 90 89 88 87 86 85

Acknowledgments

The following people reviewed the materials and provided valuable comments to the authors.

Texas

Highland Park Independent School District
Ellen Joslin, Dallas

Midway Independent School District
Nancy Little, Midway Middle School, Waco

Richardson Independent School District
Frank E. Piasecki, Ph.D., Richardson

Region XIII
Susan Adams Pennington, Computer Consultant, Education Service Center, Austin

California

Alamita Unified School District
Dian L. Haynes, Alamita

EQUALS in Computer Technology, Lawrence Hall of Science
Helen Joseph, Computer Education Specialist, University of California, Berkeley

Oakland Unified School District
Joyce Somerwill, Oakland

The following people, all of whom have classroom teaching experience, participated in testing and evaluation of the materials.

Bruce Clarke
William Farancz
Cary Langston
Mary Lou Simo
Ray Simon

Contents

Part A

Overview of AppleWorks

Part A of this book is a short introduction to the AppleWorks program. This program allows you to work with three different kinds of information: ordinary text, collections of data, and tables of numbers.

Word processing Using the computer to work with ordinary text, such as letters, book reports, or term papers, is called word processing. The word processing part of AppleWorks helps you enter text into the computer, make corrections and additions to the text, and finally print it neatly on paper. Part B of this book is about the word processor program.

Data bases Collections of data, such as telephone numbers, mailing lists, and library card catalogs, are often called data bases. Another part of AppleWorks helps you create data bases, make changes and additions, search for information, and finally print reports on paper. Data base use is the topic of Part C of this book.

Spreadsheets A lot of human labor goes into tables of numbers, such as checkbooks, budgets, and expense records. Often, such tables are written by hand on large pieces of ruled paper called spreadsheets. The spreadsheet part of AppleWorks helps you create spreadsheets, do all the necessary arithmetic, make changes and corrections, and then print the tables on paper. Part D is devoted to this subject.

Common features Each of these labor-saving computer applications is different from the others, but they all have things in common. In every case, you must start the computer with AppleWorks, learn to give commands, enter information into the computer, save and recall information on disks, and the like. Part A is an introduction to these common features of all three applications. You will use everything you learn here again and again throughout this book.

1 Application Programs

- Know the role of hardware and software in a computer system.
- Know the difference between a general-purpose programming language and an application language.
- Understand the purpose of word processor, data base, and spreadsheet software.
- Know what a computer file is.

▪ Hardware and Software

When you look at any computer system, you see boxes containing wires, switches, electrical circuits, motors, monitors, and hundreds of other parts. These parts, known as **hardware**, go together to make up the machine we call a computer. This amazing machine, however, can do nothing by itself. No matter how fancy the hardware, a computer does nothing on its own. It needs someone to give it instructions.

The role of the program All computers are designed to do one thing and one thing only: to carry out instructions. Some person must write these instructions as a **computer program**—a set of instructions in a form the computer can understand. (Programs are also called **software**.) The program must say exactly what the computer is to do, since the computer itself has no imagination or understanding.

Differences among applications The same computer hardware may be applied in thousands of different ways. It can compute the orbit of a spacecraft, find the shortest path for a traveling salesperson to take, search through a mailing list, help with writing tasks, do complicated arithmetic, and play games. The one thing that makes all these applications different from one another is the program that the computer happens to be running. If you change the software, the application changes.

▪ Computer Languages

The purpose of learning about computers is to become **computer literate**. This means more than just knowing facts about computers. It also means gaining new skills that allow you to use the computer to solve problems. *In short, you are computer literate if you can tell the computer to do the things you want it to do.*

Literacy and language To be able to tell the computer what to do, you must know a language. You must be able to use this language to express your ideas and give your instructions to the computer. There are two main types of computer **programming languages**. **General-purpose programming languages** allow you to instruct the computer to do anything it is capable of. **Application languages** are much more limited, but they make it easy for you to use the computer for a single application.

Programming languages   Logo, BASIC, and Pascal are examples of general-purpose programming languages. Using any one of them, a programmer can create all the software mentioned earlier: software for computing satellite orbits, solving business problems, playing games, and thousands of other activities. In fact, the software you will be using in the coming weeks was written in a general-purpose programming language.

Application languages   Programs for processing text, using data bases, and working with spreadsheets also require the user of the programs to know a language. These specialized languages are examples of application languages. To change a word you entered into a word processor, you must know what command to give. To search for information in a data base, you must know the right command. To add numbers on a spreadsheet, you must enter the correct instruction.

An important difference   Each application language is made up of commands and instructions. This is also true of general-purpose programming languages. But there is an important difference. The commands and instructions of an application language only make sense for that one application. For example, you cannot use a spreadsheet language to write a program that tells the computer to draw a picture or play music. But you can use a general-purpose programming language to do those things, *as well as to create the spreadsheet program itself.*

▪ Application Programs in This Book

Throughout the rest of this book, you will be using three application programs. First, you will learn the special application language for each program. Then you will use those commands and instructions to tell the computer what you want done. Each of these application programs is part of a software package called **AppleWorks**.

Word processing   The first application helps you with the job of writing letters, papers, lab reports, and the like. All these jobs deal with words on paper, so this task is called **word processing**. You will learn how to enter words into the computer and use the computer to correct errors and make changes. You will also learn how to move a whole sentence or paragraph from one place to another. Then you will find out how to tell the computer to make an exact printed copy of the finished piece of writing. Last, you will use these tools to carry out a few writing projects of your own.

Data bases   The second application helps you with the job of organizing a collection of information and searching through it. Such collections of information are called **data bases**. You will learn how to enter your information into a computer data base. You will find out how to make corrections and changes in the data. You will discover how to tell the computer to search the data base for a particular piece of information. Then you will learn how to have the computer print a report based on the information in the data base. Last, you will use these tools to create a data base of your own.

Spreadsheets   The third application helps you with the job of working with tables of numbers, called **spreadsheets**. You will find out how to enter numbers into the spreadsheet, how to fix errors, and how to make changes. You will learn how to add a whole column of numbers automatically. Then you will discover ways to have the computer move a row or column of numbers from one place to another. You will learn how to get a printed version of a spreadsheet. Last, you will use these tools to make a spreadsheet of your own.

▪ Working with Files

If you walk into the office at your school, or into any business office, you will see file cabinets. Each drawer in the cabinet contains information, but it is not just stuffed in at random. Instead, the information is organized by subject into groups of pages. Each group is in a separate manila file folder. Finding information begins by locating the proper file folder, bringing it to a desk, and then working through the information in the file.

Computer files   In the same way, information in a computer system is also stored in **files**. These files are not manila folders, of course, but they serve the same purpose: to hold a set of information of the same kind. Nor are there file cabinets in a computer system. Instead, computer files are stored on thin plastic disks covered with a magnetic layer. Information is written on the disk by putting patterns in the outer magnetic layer. The computer reads the information in exactly the same way that a videotape player gets information from a videotape.

The computer desktop   To work with an ordinary file, you must first take it from its file drawer and bring it to your desk. In the same way, to work with a computer file, you must first take it from the disk and bring it into the computer. To remind you of this similarity, the AppleWorks command for bringing a disk file into the computer's memory is Add files to the Desktop.

Saving the file   Once a file is on the Desktop—that is, in the computer's memory—you can look at the contents of the file and add or remove information from the file. When you finish work on an ordinary file, you must take it from your desktop and put it back in its file drawer. In the same way, when you finish work on a computer file, you must take it from the computer's memory and put it back on the disk. As you might guess, the AppleWorks command for this is `Save Desktop files to disk`.

Session 2 In the next session, you will be at the computer. First, you will start the computer, load the AppleWorks software, and run it. Then you will spend the rest of your time learning the commands for handling computer files. You will use these file commands again and again, whether you are doing word processing, searching a data base, or creating a spreadsheet.

QUESTIONS

1. What does the term "computer hardware" mean?
2. What is a computer program?
3. What allows the same computer to be used for several different applications?
4. What does it mean to be computer literate?
5. Why does a computer-literate person need to know a computer language?
6. What is the difference between a general-purpose programming language and an application language?
7. What three application programs will you learn about in this book?
8. What is a computer file?
9. Where are computer files usually stored?
10. What must you do with a computer file before you can work with the information in the file?
11. What must you do with a computer file after you have finished working on the information in the file?

2 Getting Started

SESSION GOALS:
- Start the computer with AppleWorks.
- Give menu commands.
- Create a new file and enter information into it.
- Save a file on a disk and move a file from a disk into memory.
- See a disk directory, delete a file from a disk, and delete a file from memory.
- Leave AppleWorks and switch the computer off.

Starting AppleWorks

You may have separate instructions for starting your Apple computer system. If so, follow those instructions. If not, follow the instructions below.

■ How to Start Your Computer with AppleWorks

This session, like all other even-numbered sessions, is a hands-on activity. You should be seated at the computer and ready to carry out the steps given below.

Before doing anything else, take a close look at your computer system hardware. It has three important parts. The main unit has a **keyboard** like the one on a typewriter. Either to one side or on top of the main unit is a display screen called a **monitor**. A TV set may be used as a monitor. Your system also has a **disk drive** either in the main unit or in a separate cabinet. The drive is behind a long horizontal slot covered by a latch. In a moment, you will be putting a disk into this slot. (If your computer has two drives, you will use the one labeled Drive 1.)

Step 1. Be sure the monitor or TV set is turned on. If there is a volume control, turn it down.

Step 2. Put the (CAPS LOCK) key in the up position. The key is at the lower left corner of the keyboard.

Step 3. Insert the disk labeled "AppleWorks Startup" into the disk drive. Follow the instructions below:

1. Open the latch in front of the disk drive slot.
2. Hold the disk with your thumb on the label, label side up.
3. Gently slide the disk all the way into the slot.
4. Close the latch slowly and tightly.

There are two ways to carry out the next step. Use step 4a if the computer power is switched off. Use step 4b if the power is already on.

Step 4a. If the computer's power light is off, just turn the power switch on. Otherwise, go to step 4b.

The power switch is at the left rear of the computer. After you switch it on, the power light on the main unit will come on.

Step 4b. If the computer is already switched on, follow the instructions below:

1. Hold down the (CONTROL) key. It is at the left end of the keyboard.
2. While the (CONTROL) key is down, hold down the (ᗑ) key just left of the spacebar. Use your left hand to hold down both keys.
3. While both keys are down, tap the (RESET) key. On the Apple IIe, this key is at the upper right corner of the keyboard. On the IIc, it is at the left above the keyboard.
4. Release all keys that you are holding down.

Whether you use step 4a or step 4b, the disk drive's red light will come on now. This tells you that the computer is reading the first part of the AppleWorks program from the disk into memory. When the disk drive light goes out, your screen should look like this:

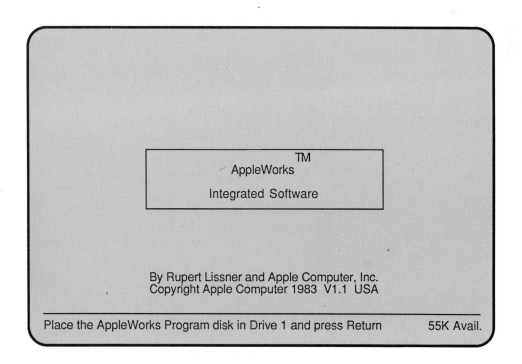

```
                          TM
                   AppleWorks

                 Integrated Software




         By Rupert Lissner and Apple Computer, Inc.
         Copyright Apple Computer 1983  V1.1  USA

Place the AppleWorks Program disk in Drive 1 and press Return    55K Avail.
```

The flashing rectangle at the bottom of the screen is called the **cursor**. Its purpose is to call your attention to the instructions printed there. These instructions lead to step 5.

Step 5. Remove the disk from the drive. Follow the directions in step 3, but this time insert the disk labeled "AppleWorks Program." Be sure to close the disk drive latch slowly.

Step 6. Tap the (RETURN) key at the right end of the keyboard.

Now the computer reads the final part of the AppleWorks program from the disk you just inserted. When the disk drive light goes out, your screen should look similar to this:

```
Files: None                 GETTING STARTED
_____




                    The date must be 1983 or later,
                    and in this form :  3/20/84




_____
Type today's date or press Return:  9/15/85              55K Avail.
```

As before, the flashing cursor is at the bottom line, calling attention to the instructions there.

Step 7. Type today's date in the form shown. Use the spacebar to remove any extra numbers.

If you make a typing error, you can use the (DELETE) key to erase characters. The computer adds the date to any information you save on your disk.

Step 8. Tap the (RETURN) key.

The computer writes your new date on the disk. Then your screen should change to look like this:

```
Disk: Drive 1                    MAIN MENU

    ┌─Main Menu──────┐──────────────────────────┐
    │                                            │
    │     1.  Add files to the Desktop           │
    │                                            │
    │     2.  Work with one of the files on the Desktop │
    │                                            │
    │     3.  Save Desktop files to disk         │
    │                                            │
    │     4.  Remove files from the Desktop      │
    │                                            │
    │     5.  Other Activities                   │
    │                                            │
    │     6.  Quit                               │
    │                                            │
    └────────────────────────────────────────────┘

 Type number, or use arrows, then press Return        ⌂-? for Help
```

This screen is called the **Main Menu**. When you see the Main Menu, you know you have started AppleWorks correctly. Now you are ready to start using the AppleWorks program.

1. When you start AppleWorks, which disk should be in the drive first?
2. After you enter the date, what menu appears on the screen next?

▪ Selecting Menu Commands

If you have used a computer before to write programs, you probably gave the computer commands by typing the name of the command on the keyboard and then pressing the (RETURN) key. To use AppleWorks, you also need to give commands, but you do it differently.

Many AppleWorks commands are contained on **menus**. You give a menu command by **selecting** a menu item and then pressing the (RETURN) key. Whenever a menu item is selected, it is **highlighted**—the letters appear as black against a bright rectangle. At the present time, item 1 on the Main Menu is selected.

Read the bottom line on the screen.

Tap the (4) key.

You have just selected menu item 4.

Tap the ⬇ key.

Now menu item 5 is selected.

Tap the ⬆ key twice.

Menu item 3 is selected.

Tap the ⬇ key until the last item on the menu is selected.

Tap the ⬇ key once more.

This wraparound effect is a quick way to get from the bottom of a menu to the top. Similarly, the ⬆ key takes you from the top menu item to the bottom one.

3. How to you know which command in a menu is selected?

4. How do you select a different menu command?

▪ Giving Menu Commands

So far, you have seen how to select a command on a menu. Next, you will see how to give the command that you have selected.

If item 1 on the menu is not highlighted, select it now.

Tap the RETURN key.

That is all it takes to give a menu command once you have selected it. In this case, the command was to Add files to the Desktop. The effect of this command is to show a new menu. Your screen should look like the one on page 11.

```
┌─ Main Menu ─────────────────────────────┐
│ ┌─ Add Files ──────────────────┐        │
│ │                              │        │
│ │     Get files from:          │        │
│ │                              │        │
│ │     1.  The current disk: Drive 1      │
│ │     2.  A different disk      │        │
│ │                              │        │
│ │     Make a new file for the:  │        │
│ │                              │        │
│ │     3. ◀Word Processor         │        │
│ │     4.  Data Base             │        │
│ │     5.  Spreadsheet           │        │
│ │                              │        │
│ │                              │        │
│ │                              │        │
│ │                              │        │
└─┴──────────────────────────────┴────────┘
```

Type number, or use arrows, then press Return   55K Avail.

The new Add Files menu appears. The top item on the new menu is already selected. You select other menu items on the new menu just as you did on the Main Menu. This is true for all AppleWorks menus.

Without tapping the (RETURN) key, use the number keys and arrow keys to practice selecting menu commands.

5. How do you give a menu command?

6. What does the Add files command on the Main Menu do?

▪ Changing Your Mind

You are now looking at the five possible commands on the Add Files menu. Suppose that you do not want to give any of these commands. Instead, you want to get back to the Main Menu and do something else.

Read the top line on the screen.

The last part of the line says Escape: Main Menu.

Tap the (ESC) key at the upper left corner of the keyboard.

The (ESC) key is known as the escape key. In AppleWorks, you go from the current menu to the previous menu when you tap this key. That is why you are now back at the Main Menu.

Read the top line on the screen.

Tap the (ESC) **key.**

The beep reminds you that the key you pressed has no meaning here. In this case, there is no previous menu. You can go only forward from the Main Menu.

Select menu item 5 and press (RETURN).

You have now given the Other Activities command. This command causes a new menu to appear.

Tap the (ESC) **key.**

Now you are back at the Main Menu.

Give the Quit **command, and then use the** (ESC) **key to return to the Main Menu.**

These exercises show you how to give a menu command and how to change your mind and go back to the previous menu.

7. How do you get back to a previous menu in AppleWorks?
8. What happens if you tap the (ESC) key while at the Main Menu?

▪ Entering Information into the Computer

The purpose of AppleWorks is to help you enter information into the computer and then work with that information. The information is stored in blocks called **files**. The first four commands on the Main Menu tell the computer to do something to or with these files.

Read command 2 on the Main Menu.

This command tells the computer that you want to work with a file that is on the Desktop. When there is a file of information in the computer's **memory**, the file is said to be on the Desktop.

Give command 2 on the Main Menu.

The message in the middle of the screen tells you that there are no files on the Desktop. Let us create one.

Go back to the Main Menu and give command 1.

You have seen the Add Files menu before. The first two commands tell the computer to get files that are stored on a disk. The last three commands tell the computer to create a new file. These three commands show that the new file can be a word processor file, a data base file, or a spreadsheet file. Begin with the word processor file.

Tell the computer to create a new word processor file.

A third menu is now on the screen. The new menu asks whether you want to make the new file from scratch or from an existing text file. From scratch means that you want a new file with nothing in it.

Give menu command 1 to create a new file From scratch.

At this point, your screen should look like this:

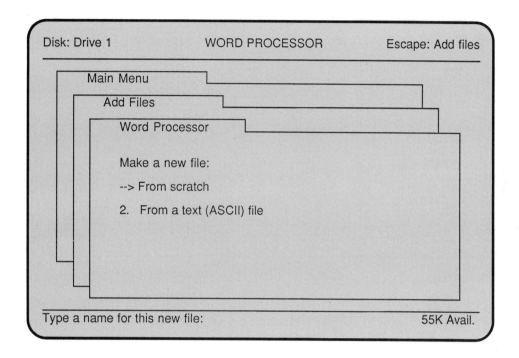

```
Disk: Drive 1              WORD PROCESSOR          Escape: Add files
─────────────────────────────────────────────────────────────────
    ┌─ Main Menu ─────────────────────────────────────────┐
    │ ┌─ Add Files ──────────────────────────────────────┐│
    │ │ ┌─ Word Processor ──────────────────────────────┐││
    │ │ │                                               │││
    │ │ │   Make a new file:                            │││
    │ │ │   --> From scratch                            │││
    │ │ │   2.  From a text (ASCII) file                │││
    │ │ │                                               │││
    │ │ │                                               │││
    │ │ │                                               │││
    └─┴─┴───────────────────────────────────────────────┴┴┘
  Type a name for this new file:                      55K Avail.
```

Type the name MyText. **Use the** ⟨DELETE⟩ **key to erase mistakes.**

When the name is correct, tap ⟨RETURN⟩.

When you finish, the screen should look like this:

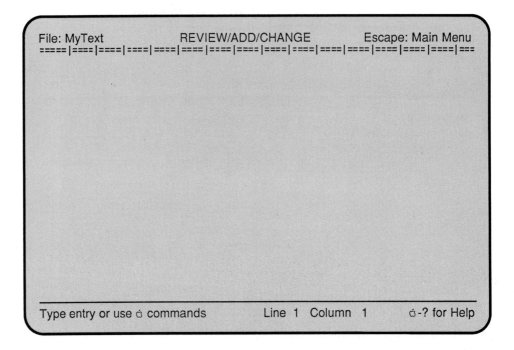

There are no menus here. Instead, you have reached a screen with REVIEW/ADD/CHANGE at the top. Any time you see this label at the top of a screen, the computer is waiting for you to enter information.

Read the prompt line at the bottom of the screen.

The computer tells you either to type an entry or use Open-Apple (ᬗ) commands. (You will learn about Open-Apple commands later.) Whatever you type now will be stored in the file named MyText.

Type the sentence below. Use the (DELETE) key to erase any mistakes.

I am using a computer to type this sentence.

As you type each letter, the cursor moves to the right, and the column number at the bottom of the screen changes.

Tap the (RETURN) key twice.

You are now at line 3, column 1.

Type your name.

You could go on adding hundreds or thousands of words to this file. However, you can use this small file to learn how to save the information on your disk and get it back.

9. If you are at the Main Menu, what steps are necessary to create a new word processor file?

10. What screen allows you to enter information into a file?

▪ Saving Files

At the present time, the file you have created is in the computer's memory. If you turned off the power to the computer, the information would be lost. To put a copy of the file on your disk you need to use a command on the Main Menu.

Read the message at the upper right corner of the screen. Then tap the ⌜ESC⌟ key.

You are now back at the Main Menu. You may be wondering if you lost the information you entered.

Again, read the message at the upper right corner of the screen. Then tap the ⌜ESC⌟ key.

Nothing is lost. You can use the ⌜ESC⌟ key to toggle back and forth between the REVIEW/ADD/CHANGE screen and the Main Menu.

Go back to the Main Menu.

The third command is the one you need to move a copy of your file to your disk.

Give command 3 on the Main Menu.

The result is the Save Files menu, which looks like this:

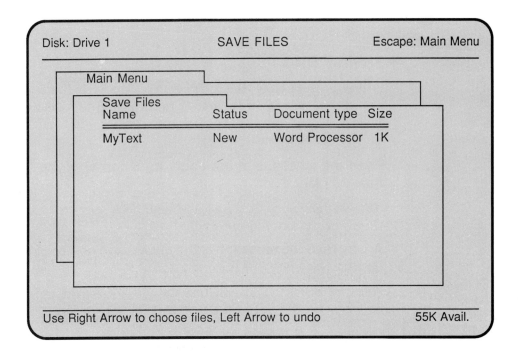

MyText is the only file now on the Desktop, so it is the only name that appears on the Save Files menu. Since the file name is highlighted, you need only tap (RETURN) to tell the computer you want the file saved.

Tap the (RETURN) key.

Now there is a third menu on the screen shown on page 17:

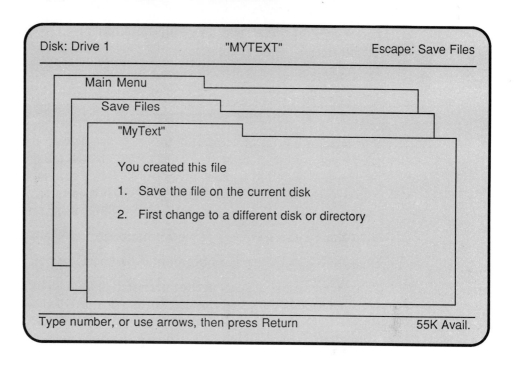

```
Disk: Drive 1                    "MYTEXT"              Escape: Save Files
─────────────────────────────────────────────────────────────────────
   ┌─ Main Menu ──────────────────────────────────────────────┐
   │  ┌─ Save Files ─────────────────────────────────────────┐ │
   │  │  ┌─ "MyText" ──────────────────────────────────────┐ │ │
   │  │  │                                                  │ │ │
   │  │  │   You created this file                          │ │ │
   │  │  │   1.  Save the file on the current disk          │ │ │
   │  │  │   2.  First change to a different disk or        │ │ │
   │  │  │       directory                                  │ │ │
   │  │  │                                                  │ │ │
   │  │  │                                                  │ │ │
   │  │  │                                                  │ │ │
   │  │  │                                                  │ │ │
─────────────────────────────────────────────────────────────────────
Type number, or use arrows, then press Return          55K Avail.
```

We will assume that you have only one disk drive. (If you have two disk drives or are using a network, you may have separate instructions for what to do now.)

Command 1 may not look like the right choice, but it is. You will see why in a minute.

Give command 1. Then read the bottom line on the screen.

As usual, the message at the bottom of the screen tells you what to do.

Remove the AppleWorks Program Disk from the drive and insert your Computer Applications DATA Disk. Then tap (RETURN).

The red disk drive light comes on, showing that the computer is saving a copy of the file MyText on the disk. The original version of the file is still in the computer's memory. After the file is saved, the computer returns to the Main Menu.

11. Which menu contains the Save files command?

12. What does saving a file mean?

13. Where on the screen does the computer prompt you about what to do next?

14. After you save a file, it is on your disk. Where else is it?

▪ Looking at a Disk Directory

If you have used the computer to write programs, you have probably used a command such as CATALOG or DIR to see a list of files on a disk. Such a list is called a **disk directory**. You can also see a directory of AppleWorks files on your Computer Applications DATA Disk. The directory command is on a menu.

Give the Other Activities **command on the Main Menu.**

Give the List all files **command on the Other Activities menu.**

That causes a list of files on the current disk to be displayed. You should see the name MyText in the list. Notice that the type of the file is Word Processor and that its size is 1K, which stands for 1024 characters. Even though you did not type this many characters, the smallest possible file size is 1K. Last, notice that the date is the same one you entered when you started AppleWorks.

Tap (ESC) **twice to get back to the Main Menu.**

15. Which menu contains the command for showing the directory of a disk?

16. What information about a file does a disk directory contain?

▪ Clearing the Desktop

Although you saved a copy of file MyText on your disk, the original is still on the Desktop—that is, it is still in the computer's memory. There is no harm in leaving a file on the Desktop, but it can be confusing when there are too many files there. It is always a good idea to remove a file from the Desktop as soon as you are finished working with it.

Give the Remove files **command on the Main Menu.**

A menu is displayed, showing you all files on the Desktop. You have only one, and it is already selected. If there were several files on the Desktop, you could select one or more of them to be removed.

Tap (RETURN).

The file is removed from the Desktop, and you are returned to the Main Menu. You can easily confirm that the Desktop is now cleared.

Give the Work with files **command on the Main Menu.**

The boxed message at the center of the screen tells you that the Desktop is cleared.

Go back to the Main Menu.

17. What menu contains the command for removing a file from the Desktop?

18. What does it mean to remove a file from the Desktop?

▪ Getting a File from a Disk

The file MyText that you created is no longer on the Desktop, but a copy is still on your disk. If you have used a computer before, you may have typed a command such as LOAD or GET to move a copy of a file from a disk into the computer's memory. AppleWorks has a menu command to do the same thing.

Give the Add files command on the Main Menu.

Give command 1 on the Add Files menu.

Follow the instructions as they appear at the bottom of the screen. When prompted, swap disks until you see a directory on the screen.

The AppleWorks files menu shows you a directory of all the files on your disk. For now, ignore the prompt at the bottom of the screen.

Use the ⬇ key to select MyText. Then tap RETURN.

The red disk drive light comes on, telling you that the computer is moving a copy of MyText onto the Desktop. When the move is complete, you see the REVIEW/ADD/CHANGE screen and the contents of file MyText that you entered earlier in this session. If you wished, you could now add, change, or delete information from this file and then save the new version back on the disk. You will learn more about these things in Session 4.

19. What steps are necessary to move a copy of a file from your disk into the computer's memory?

20. If you need to swap disks, where do the instructions appear on the screen?

▪ Removing a File from the Disk

Once again, identical copies of file MyText appear in two places: on the Desktop and on your disk. You will see next how to remove the copy on the disk.

Go back to the Main Menu.

Give the Other Activities **command on the Main Menu.**

Give the Delete files **command on the Other Activities menu.**

Once again, you see the directory of your disk. The computer is waiting for you to select the file you wish to delete.

Select MyText **and tap** (RETURN).

At the bottom of the screen, the computer asks if you *really* want to do this. If you tap (Y), the file will be erased permanently from the disk.

Tap the (Y) **key to confirm that you do want to delete the file.**

The red disk drive light comes on as the computer erases file MyText from the disk. After that, AppleWorks returns to the Other Activities menu.

Give the List all files **command on the Other Activities menu.**

The new directory shows that file MyText is no longer on the disk.

Tap (ESC) **twice to get back to the Main Menu.**

Give command 2 on the Main Menu.

That returns you directly to the REVIEW/ADD/CHANGE screen. Are you surprised to see the copy of file MyText still on the Desktop? The disk copy is gone, but the Desktop copy is still in the computer's memory. If necessary, you could save a copy of MyText on the disk again.

21. What menu contains the command for deleting a file from a disk?

22. What does it mean to delete a file from a disk?

▪ Quitting AppleWorks

In this session you have done all of the things you will be doing again and again when using AppleWorks. Now it is time to learn how to leave AppleWorks in an orderly way. The first step is to clear the Desktop of all files.

Return to the Main Menu.

Give the Remove files **command on the Main Menu.**

The only file on the Desktop should be MyText, and it should already be selected.

Tap (RETURN).

If you have changed a file since you last saved it, the computer will ask you what you want to do with the new version.

If prompted, tell the computer to throw away the changes in file MyText.

That clears the Desktop. (If you had several files on the Desktop, you could remove each one the same way.)

Give the Quit **command on the Main Menu.**

The prompt at the bottom of the screen asks you if you really mean what you said. If you had selected the Quit command by accident, you could change your mind at this point.

Tap the (Y) **key to confirm that you do want to quit.**

If you are using one drive, you will be prompted to swap your Computer Applications DATA Disk with the AppleWorks Program Disk.

If necessary, swap disks and tap (RETURN).

The ENTER PREFIX message at the top of the screen means that the AppleWorks program is no longer running in the computer.

Remove the AppleWorks Program Disk from the drive. Return it and the AppleWorks Startup Disk to their proper location.

Take your Computer Applications DATA Disk with you.

When you leave the computer, it is a good idea to leave the computer on if someone else will be using it within an hour or so. You should, however, turn down the brightness control on the monitor or TV screen. This precaution extends the life of the screen.

23. What steps should you follow when quitting AppleWorks?
24. Why does the computer ask you if you really want to quit?

If you have time:

ON YOUR OWN

- Practice restarting the computer with AppleWorks and quitting AppleWorks.

- Restart AppleWorks. Use the Add files command on the Main Menu to look at other files on your Computer Applications DATA Disk. When you are through looking at each file, remove it from the Desktop. *Do not use the* Save Desktop *command.*

- Create a new word processor file. Give it any name you choose. Enter any information you want into the file. Practice saving the file on your disk, looking at the disk directory, deleting the file from the disk, and removing the file from the Desktop.

  When you finish these activities, be sure to quit AppleWorks as shown earlier.

3 The AppleWorks Package

SESSION GOALS: • Understand where information is stored in a computer system.
• Review the steps for starting and quitting AppleWorks.
• Review the steps for creating, saving, loading, and deleting files.

▪ Where Is the Information?

Working with computers is working with information. Whenever you do any computer work, it is important to know exactly where the information is. Is it on the disk? Is it in the computer's memory? Is it both places? Is it neither place? Not knowing the answer to these questions is the main cause of confusion and lost information.

Files In AppleWorks, information is grouped together into units called *files*, as you saw earlier. A letter you write can be in one file, a book report in another file, and an arithmetic table in a third file. The AppleWorks program moves a whole file at a time between the disk and the memory of the computer. Therefore, knowing where your information is means knowing where your files are.

Disk files It is easy to find out what files are on a disk. You simply ask AppleWorks to show you the disk directory. (See page 26 for the steps.) If the name of the file you are interested in is in the directory, the file is safely on the disk. The information in a disk file remains there after you switch the computer power off.

Files in memory The other place a file can be is in the computer's *memory*. Such a file is not as safe as one on a disk. When electrical power is switched off, everything in memory is erased.

The Desktop When a file is in the memory of the computer, it is said to be on the AppleWorks *Desktop*. You can see what files are in memory by going to the Main Menu and giving any command that refers to the Desktop. The first thing the computer will do is display a list of the names of all files in memory. After that, you can use the ⎡ESC⎤ key to cancel the command.

Loading a file into memory When you use the steps on page 26 to get a file from the disk, the file itself is not moved. Instead, the computer makes a copy of the disk file and puts the copy in memory (on the Desktop). The original remains safely on the disk. The only way to remove the file from the disk is by using the `Delete files` command on the Other Activities menu.

Saving a file on the disk This works the same way. When you save a file, the computer makes a copy of the file in memory and writes the copy on the disk. The original is still in memory. The only way to remove a file from memory (except for switching the power off) is by using the `Remove files from the Desktop` command on the Main Menu.

More than one file in memory If you have used a computer for programming, you probably were unable to have more than one file in memory at the same time. Each new file erased the old one. This is not true of AppleWorks. Adding a new file has no effect on files already in memory. You will not be using this feature of AppleWorks in these sessions. However, you should know about the feature in case you accidentally add a file to the Desktop before removing an old one.

■ Starting the Computer with AppleWorks

In Session 2, you learned the main things you need to know to use the AppleWorks program. Now is a good time to review what you did. These pages will be a good place to return to when you want a quick reminder of the steps needed to perform a common task.

The parts of the computer system The computer you used has three main hardware parts. The *main unit* contains a keyboard and most of the electrical circuits. The computer's memory is in the main unit. The *monitor* shows information coming from the computer. The *disk drive* holds the thin plastic disks that the computer uses to store information. All these parts make up the complete computer system.

The AppleWorks disks As you learned in Session 1, no computer system works without a *program*, which is a set of instructions to tell the computer exactly what to do. AppleWorks comes in two main pieces. The first part is on the AppleWorks Startup Disk, and the second part is on the AppleWorks Program Disk. To start using AppleWorks, you first had to load both parts of the AppleWorks software into your computer's memory.

Starting the computer You start the computer with AppleWorks by carrying out these steps:

1. Turn on the monitor.
2. Put the AppleWorks Startup Disk in the drive.
3. Either switch the power on or type the [CONTROL | ⓒ | RESET] key combination.
4. Follow the instructions on the screen to insert the AppleWorks Program Disk in the drive. Then tap [RETURN].
5. Follow the instructions on the screen to type today's date. Then tap [RETURN].

These steps cause the computer to place the AppleWorks program in its memory and to start the program running. From then until the end of the session, AppleWorks is in charge of your computer.

■ The Main Menu

After starting AppleWorks, the first thing you see is the Main Menu. It looks like this:

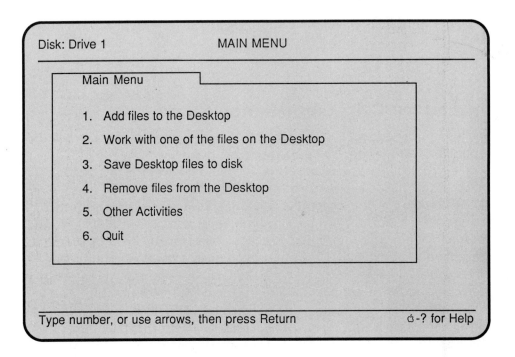

```
Disk: Drive 1                    MAIN MENU
─────────────────────────────────────────────────────
 ┌─ Main Menu ──────────┐
 │                                                    │
 │    1.   Add files to the Desktop                   │
 │                                                    │
 │    2.   Work with one of the files on the Desktop  │
 │                                                    │
 │    3.   Save Desktop files to disk                 │
 │                                                    │
 │    4.   Remove files from the Desktop              │
 │                                                    │
 │    5.   Other Activities                           │
 │                                                    │
 │    6.   Quit                                       │
 │                                                    │
 └────────────────────────────────────────────────────┘

─────────────────────────────────────────────────────
Type number, or use arrows, then press Return      ⌂-? for Help
```

Information on the screen Whenever you are confused, always look at the top and bottom lines of the screen before doing anything else. The top line always tells where you are in AppleWorks. (It may also tell you where you will be if you tap the (ESC) key.) The bottom screen line tells what needs to be done next. For example, the message at the bottom of the Main Menu tells you how to enter a command.

Menu commands The Main Menu is a list of six commands that you can give to the computer. If you have written programs on a computer, you probably gave commands by typing the name of the command. AppleWorks commands are different. You give an AppleWorks command by first *selecting* it from a menu and then tapping the (RETURN) key. You select a command by typing its number or by using the arrow keys to move down or up the menu. Selected commands always appear highlighted, that is, in black type on a bright background. You can change your mind about most commands, even after tapping $\boxed{\text{RETURN}}$, by tapping the $\boxed{\text{ESC}}$ key.

▪ Working with Files

The purpose of AppleWorks is to help you enter information into the computer and work with it. A single block of information is called a *file*. Here are the steps you use to create a new word processor file:

1. Give the Add files command on the Main Menu.
2. Give the Word Processor command on the Add files menu.
3. Give the From scratch command from the Word Processor menu.
4. Type a name for the file and tap $\boxed{\text{RETURN}}$.

The REVIEW/ADD/CHANGE screen   As soon as you create the new file, the computer shows you the REVIEW/ADD/CHANGE screen. It looks like this:

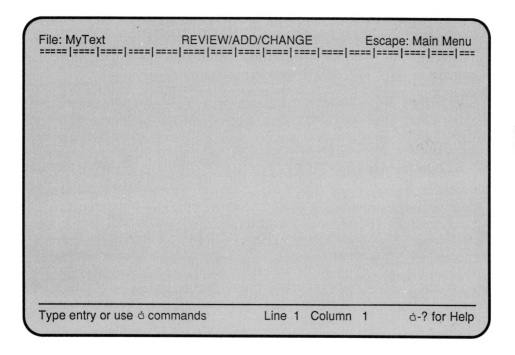

```
File: MyText          REVIEW/ADD/CHANGE          Escape: Main Menu
=====|====|====|====|====|====|====|====|====|====|====|====|====|====|===
```

```
Type entry or use ɔ́ commands          Line 1  Column  1          ɔ́-? for Help
```

This is a very important screen. In AppleWorks, whenever you are entering or working with information, you will be àt a REVIEW/ADD/ CHANGE screen. Most of your time at the computer will be spent at a screen similar to this.

Entering information For a new file, most of the REVIEW/ADD/ CHANGE screen is blank, since the file is empty. You enter information simply by typing it on the keyboard. As you type each letter, it appears on the screen at the location of the flashing cursor. You can fix typing errors with the (DELETE) key.

Saving the file After entering the information into your file, you save it by using these steps:

1. Tap (ESC) to return to the Main Menu.
2. Give the Save Desktop command on the Main Menu.
3. Select the name of the file to be saved and tap (RETURN).
4. Give the command saying that you want the file to be saved on the current disk.
5. When prompted, swap your Computer Applications DATA Disk with the AppleWorks Program Disk in the drive. Then tap (RETURN).

The disk directory The disk *directory* is the place on the disk that contains information about all files on the disk. You look at your disk directory by using these steps:

1. Go to the Main Menu.
2. Give the Other Activities command.
3. Give the List all files command.

The directory display shows the name, type, size, and date of each file on your disk. When you start the computer with AppleWorks, you type today's date. That's how the computer knows what date to use when you save a file.

The Other Activities menu The most frequently used commands are on the Main Menu. The next-to-last command there causes the Other Activities menu to appear. You can think of this menu as an extension of the Main Menu. You will use the Other Activities menu for only two purposes: looking at a disk directory and deleting a disk file.

Getting a file from the disk To work with information already stored on a disk, you must get its file back into the computer's memory. You use these steps to load a file into the computer:

1. Go to the Main Menu.
2. Give the Add files command.
3. Give the From the current disk command.
4. From the directory that appears, select the name of the file you want loaded. Then tap (RETURN).

The result is that you see the REVIEW/ADD/CHANGE screen. It contains part or all of the information in the file you loaded.

Deleting a file from a disk   When a file is no longer needed, you will want to remove it from the disk. You do this by following these steps:

1. Go to the Main Menu.
2. Give the `Other Activities` command.
3. Give the `Delete files` command.
4. Select the name of the file to be removed. Then tap `RETURN`.
5. Tap the `Y` key to confirm that you really do want the file to be removed.

The last step is a nice example of friendliness in using this program. The writer of this program knew that deleting a disk file is permanent. There is no way to get a deleted file back. So the writer had the program pause and ask you to make certain that the selected file should really disappear from the disk. This pause gives you a chance to change your mind before any damage is done.

Quitting AppleWorks   In Session 2, your last activity at the computer was to make an orderly exit from the AppleWorks program. Here are the steps you follow:

1. Go to the Main Menu.
2. Give the `Remove files` command and remove any files on the Desktop.
3. Give the `Quit` command on the Main Menu.
4. Tap the `Y` key to confirm that you really want to quit.
5. Remove the disk from the drive.
6. Switch the power off or turn down the brightness of the monitor or TV screen.

QUESTIONS

1. What are the three main parts of your computer system?
2. Where is the AppleWorks software stored?
3. What is the purpose of putting the AppleWorks software into the computer and running it?
4. When you start the computer, you are asked to enter the date. How does AppleWorks make use of the date?
5. Which key is always used to give a menu command?
6. Which key usually cancels the previous menu command you gave?

7. If you are at the Main Menu and want to create a new file, what is the first command you must give?

8. What does the top line on an AppleWorks screen tell you?

9. What does the bottom line on an AppleWorks screen tell you?

10. On which screen do you enter new information into a file?

11. If you are entering information into a file and decide to save the file on your disk, what is the first key you should tap?

12. Suppose you have just finished saving a file on the disk. Where else is the file?

13. What does it mean to say that a file is on the Desktop in AppleWorks?

14. What is a disk directory?

15. What command displays the disk directory? What menu is the command on?

16. Suppose you have just loaded a file into memory from a disk. Then by accident, you switch the power off. Does the file still exist anywhere? If so, where?

17. Suppose you have just saved a file on your disk. Then by accident, you delete the file from the disk. Does the file still exist anywhere? If so, where?

Part A

▪ Menu Commands

Add files   A Main Menu command for duplicating a disk file onto the Desktop or for creating new files from scratch.

Delete files   An Other Activities menu command for erasing a file permanently from a disk.

List all files   An Other Activities menu command for displaying the directory of files on a disk.

Other Activities   A Main Menu command that extends the list of commands available. The new commands appear on a menu headed Other Activities.

Quit   A Main Menu command for quitting AppleWorks.

Remove files   A Main Menu command for erasing the copy of a file in the computer's memory. The disk copy, if any, is not affected.

Save Desktop   A Main Menu command for duplicating, onto a disk, a file in the computer's memory.

Word Processor   An Add Files menu command to create a new file for use with the word processor program.

Work with files   A Main Menu command to continue working with a file already in the computer's memory.

▪ Keyboard Commands

(DELETE)   Erase the character just left of the cursor position.

(ESC)   In most cases, undo the effect of the previous command and return to the menu the command was on.

(RETURN)   In most cases, issue a command or mark the end of an entry. When entering text into a word processor file, (RETURN) is used to end a paragraph or enter a blank line.

(ɕ)   Not actually a command. This key is used with other keys to give special commands.

(↑), (↓)   Move the cursor up or down a line in a word processor file.

(→), (←)   Move the cursor right or left one character in a word processor file.

▪ New Ideas

AppleWorks   A package of computer programs that allows you to work with lists of information, write documents, and manipulate numbers.

application language   A language designed for a particular purpose, such as editing text, organizing data, and making routine calculations.

computer literate   Able to tell the computer how to do what you want it to do.

computer program   A set of instructions in a form the computer can understand.

data base program   A computer program that helps you organize, search through, and manipulate a collection of information.

disk directory   A list of files on a disk.

disk drive   Computer hardware that can store information on and retrieve information from a disk with a magnetic coating.

file   A collection of information. Computer files are stored on disks from which they can be retrieved as needed.

hardware   The wires, switches, chips, electrical circuits, motors, monitors or TV screens, and other parts that make up a computer.

keyboard   A typewriter-like device used to send information to the computer.

memory   A part of the computer hardware where information can be stored temporarily.

menu   A list of commands that can be given.

monitor   A screen unit upon which information is displayed.

programming language   A general-purpose language. Examples are Logo, BASIC, and Pascal. Application programs are written using programming languages like these.

save a file   Duplicate a copy of a file that is in the computer's memory onto a disk.

select   Move the cursor to an AppleWorks command name. Selected commands are highlighted.

software   Another word for computer programs.

spreadsheet program   A computer program that helps you do calculations on data stored in cells.

word processor program   A computer program that helps you enter, edit, and print text.

Part **B**

Word Processing

In Part A, you learned what an application program is. You also learned that the AppleWorks software package contains three different application programs. There is one for word processing, one for working with data bases, and one for building spreadsheets.

Common features Although each application is different, they all have things in common. Part A introduced you to these common features. You learned how to start the computer with AppleWorks, how to give commands, and how to enter information into the computer. You learned that information is stored in files. You found out how to create an empty file, how to save a file on a disk, and how to get a file from a disk.

The writing task In Part B, you will learn the main things necessary for using the word processor in AppleWorks. This program helps you with writing tasks. The hardest part of writing, for most people, is making changes. Without a computer, that means having to erase or scratch out words and then pencil in new words. After a few changes, your paper looks messy. You may have to rewrite or retype the whole thing.

The word processor With a word processor, however, you can easily make any changes you want. You can also get a perfect copy without rewriting everything. The first step is to enter the words you write into the computer. For this step, you use the computer much as you use a typewriter. The second step is making corrections and changes. The final step is printing the improved text on paper. You will learn to do all these things in Part B.

4 Exploring the Word Processor

SESSION GOALS: • Review starting the computer with AppleWorks.
- Enter text into an empty word processor file.
- Insert and delete words in a word processor file.
- Send a copy of a word processor file to a printer.

▪ Starting AppleWorks for Word Processing

In this session, you will begin to learn about the word processor program in AppleWorks. As with every hands-on session, the first step is to start the computer with the AppleWorks disks.

Use the usual steps, shown below, to start the computer.

1. Turn on the monitor. Put the (CAPS LOCK) key in the up position.
2. Put the AppleWorks Startup disk in the drive.
3. Either switch the power on or type the (CONTROL | ⌂ | RESET) key combination.
4. When prompted, remove the AppleWorks Startup Disk from the drive. Then insert the AppleWorks Program Disk and tap (RETURN).
5. When prompted, type today's date and tap (RETURN).

If you need more information about starting the computer with AppleWorks, see pages 6–9.

If all went well, you should see the Main Menu on the screen. The first command, Add files, is already selected. There are no files on the Desktop when you start AppleWorks, so your first step in doing anything is to add a file.

Tap (RETURN) to give the Add files command.

You should see the five commands on the Add Files menu. Now it is time to decide what to do. Your first activity in this session will be to enter text into a new word processor file. It should be clear what command to use next.

Select command 3. Then give the command.

Remember that you can use the (ESC) key if you give the wrong command. Now you should see the two commands on the Word Processor menu. You will be creating a file from scratch, so command 1 is the proper choice.

Tap (RETURN) to give command 1.

As usual, the prompt at the bottom of the screen tells you what needs to be done next. To create a new file, you must give it a name.

Type the name Speech. Use the (DELETE) key to correct any typing errors. Then tap (RETURN).

All done. Your new file, named Speech, is now on the Desktop. You are at the REVIEW/ADD/CHANGE screen. The flashing cursor in the blank area of the screen tells you that the computer is waiting for you to enter information into your empty file.

1. Suppose you have just started AppleWorks. You want to enter information into a new file. What command on the Main Menu should you give?
2. What must you do to a new file before you can enter information into it?
3. How do you know that you have succeeded in creating a new file?

▪ Entering Text

Now it is time to begin using the word processor program. Your first activity will be to enter a short text passage into your file.

Type the following sentence. Be sure *not* to tap the (RETURN) key at the end of each line.

```
A number of years ago, some folks started a
country that believed people were OK.
```

If you were typing this sentence on a typewriter, you would have to watch each line and tap the (RETURN) key when the line got too long. The computer uses a process called **wordwrap**. When a word is too long to fit on the current line, the computer moves it to the beginning of the next line. The only times you will need to use the (RETURN) key while using the word processor are when you want to end a paragraph or enter a blank line.

4. How do you enter information into a word processor file?
5. Why should you *not* use the (RETURN) key while typing a paragraph into a word processor file?

■ Inserting Words

After you have written something, you usually think of ways to improve it. Normally, this means rewriting or retyping everything. With a word processor program, however, all you need to do is add new words or remove old words. No rewriting is necessary. For example, here is how to change `folks` to `pretty terrific folks` in your sentence.

Tap the ⬆ key once and the ➡ key four times. That should place the cursor under the `f` in `folks`. (If the cursor is not there, use the arrow keys to put it there.)

Type the words `pretty terrific`. (Use the (DELETE) key to fix errors.) Then tap the spacebar to add a space.

That is all there is to adding words. You simply move the cursor to the position where you want to make the addition and then type the new words. Here is how your REVIEW/ADD/CHANGE screen should look:

```
File: Speech              REVIEW/ADD/CHANGE           Escape: Main Menu
=====|====|====|====|====|====|====|====|====|====|====|====|====|====|====|===
A number of years ago, some pretty terrific folks started a
country that believed people were OK.




Type entry or use ᑖ commands        Line 2  Column 22      ᑖ-? for Help
```

Use the arrow keys to move the cursor key under the first `P` in `people`. Be sure not to use the (RETURN) key to move the cursor.

Type the word `all` and a space.

6. What keys move the cursor without affecting the words in the file?

7. How would you insert the word book just ahead of the word mark in a word processor file?

▪ Deleting Words

You have seen how to **insert** new text. Now you will see how to get rid of unwanted text. This process is called **deletion**. Here is how to delete pretty from the sentence.

Move the cursor under the space after pretty. Use the (DELETE) key to erase the word pretty and the space before it.

Again, that is all there is to it. To delete text, place the cursor just right of the last letter. Then use the (DELETE) key to erase what you want. Here is what your screen should look like now:

```
File: Speech            REVIEW/ADD/CHANGE          Escape: Main Menu
=====|====|====|====|====|====|====|====|====|====|====|====|====|====|====|===
A number of years ago, some terrific folks started a country
that believed people were OK.




















Type entry or use ḋ commands          Line 1   Column 28       ḋ-? for Help
```

8. Suppose the cursor is at the letter r in the word years. You tap the (DELETE) key once. What character is erased from your file?

9. Suppose you want to delete the word cat from a file. Where should the cursor be before you begin tapping the (DELETE) key?

▪ Changing Words

You now know how to use the main tools for editing text. You can delete words you do not want and add new words. This way, you can make changes without having to retype everything. You will be using these editing tools again and again, so this is a good time to get some practice.

Use the steps below to change `people were OK` **to** `men are created equal.`

1. Place the cursor under the period after `OK`.
2. Delete `people were OK`.
3. Type `men are created equal`.

That is all there is to changing old words to new words. You simply delete the old words and type the new words.

Use the same method to change `some terrific folks` **to** `our fathers`.

Change `that believed` **to the following phrase:**

`dedicated to the proposition that`

After these changes, your screen should look like this:

File: Speech   REVIEW/ADD/CHANGE   Escape: Main Menu
=====|====|====|====|====|====|====|====|====|====|====|====|====|====|====|===
A number of years ago, our fathers started a country
dedicated to the proposition that all men are created equal.

Type entry or use ⌂ commands   Line 1 Column 23   ⌂-? for Help

Replace `started` **by the phrase below. Remember, do not use the** `RETURN` **key.**

> `brought forth on this continent`

Replace `country` **by the following phrase:**

> `new nation, conceived in Liberty, and`

Change `A number of` **to this phrase:**

> `Four score and seven`

Use the arrow to move the cursor just after the period at the end of the sentence.

Tap the `RETURN` **key twice. Type** `Abraham Lincoln.`

After all these changes, you should now have the following familiar quotation on your screen:

```
File: Speech            REVIEW/ADD/CHANGE          Escape: Main Menu
=====|====|====|====|====|====|====|====|====|====|====|====|====|====|===
Four score and seven years ago, our fathers brought forth on
this continent a new nation, conceived in Liberty, and
dedicated to the proposition that all men are created equal.

Abraham Lincoln






_____
Type entry or use ᑌ commands        Line 5  Column 16      ᑌ-? for Help
```

If your screen does not look like this one, use insertion and deletion to correct any errors.

If necessary, move the cursor to the right of `Lincoln`**. Then tap** `RETURN` **three times. Type the following sentence:**

> `I used a word processor program to write this.`

Tap (RETURN) twice and type your name.

10. To substitute one word for another word, what two things do you need to know how to do?

11. What are the steps for substituting one phrase for another phrase?

▪ Saving the File

At this point, you have created a new word processor file named Speech. This file contains the words you see on the screen right now. However, the file exists only on the Desktop—in the computer's memory. If you switched the computer off now, your work would be lost. The safe thing to do is to put a copy of the file on your Computer Applications DATA Disk. You learned how to save files in Session 2.

Use the steps below to save the file Speech on your disk:

1. Tap (ESC) to go back to the Main Menu.
2. Give the Save Desktop command.
3. Select the name Speech and then tap (RETURN).
4. Give command 1 on the "Speech" menu.
5. Follow the instructions to swap your Computer Applications DATA Disk with the AppleWorks Program Disk in the drive. Then tap (RETURN).

When you finish these steps, the computer writes a copy of the file Speech on your disk and then returns to the Main Menu.

Tap the (ESC) key to go back to the REVIEW/ADD/CHANGE screen.

As you see, you now have two copies of file Speech. One is on your disk, and the other is still on the Desktop.

12. What menu has the Save Desktop command?

13. When the wrong disk is in the drive, the computer asks you to put in the right one. Where on the screen does the computer's message appear?

▪ Printing a File

Your word processor file is on your disk and also in the memory of the computer. Sooner or later, however, you will also want to print a copy of the file on paper. If there is a printer attached to your computer, you can make the copy right now. If not, you will have to take your Computer Applications DATA Disk to another computer that has a printer attached.

You may have special instructions for using a printer with AppleWorks. If so, follow those instructions instead of the ones below.

Use these steps to get your printer ready:

1. Be sure the printer has paper in it.
2. If the printer is not on, switch it on now.
3. If the SEL (or Select, or On Line) light is off, tap the button that turns it on.

Use the following steps to make a printed copy of file Speech:

1. Make sure your file is visible on the REVIEW/ADD/CHANGE screen.
2. Hold down the Ⓒ key and tap the Ⓟ key. Then release both keys.
3. If necessary, follow the instructions for swapping disks and then tap (RETURN).
4. Tap (RETURN) to print the whole file from the beginning.
5. Select the name of the printer you are using and then tap (RETURN).
6. Tap (RETURN) to print one copy of the file.

The printing should start immediately. If not, check the SEL (or Select, or On Line) light. If it is off, tap the button that turns it on.

When printing is over, the computer returns to the REVIEW/ADD/CHANGE screen. (There is an extra line under the information you typed, but it will go away as soon as you insert or delete anything from the file. The line is not really part of the file.)

Use these steps to remove the paper:

1. Tap the SEL (or Select, or On Line) button on your printer again.
2. Tap the TOF (or Form Feed, or FF) button.
3. Carefully tear the paper off at a perforation.
4. Tap the SEL (or Select, or On Line) button on your printer once more.

That completes all your regular activities in this session. If you have time, carry out some of the On Your Own activities below.

When you finish all your work at the computer, follow the steps on pages 20–21 for clearing your Desktop and quitting.

14. At which screen must you be to print a file?

15. What keyboard command tells the computer that you want to print a file?

If you have time:

ON YOUR OWN

- Use the Remove files command from the Main Menu to clear your Desktop. Then use the Add files command to get file Spell from your Computer Applications DATA Disk. Find all the misspelled words you can, and change each one to the correct spelling. Use the ⌧N command to change the file name to SpellOK. Use the Save Desktop command to save the improved version. Print it.

- Clear your Desktop and get file Punctuate from your Computer Applications DATA Disk. The text you see has no punctuation or capital letters. Insert whatever punctuation is needed. Capitalize any letters that need it. Use the ⌧N command to change the file name to PunctuateOK. Save the corrected version. Print it.

- Clear your Desktop. Create a new word processor file. Name the file MyThoughts. Write a few sentences that tell what you think about using a word processor program on a computer.

5 Word Processor Files

SESSION GOALS:
- Review the steps for creating a new word processor file.
- Review entering text, inserting and deleting words.
- Review the steps for saving a word processor file on a disk.
- Review the steps for sending a word processor file to the printer.
- Understand why file editing tools are the basis of all word processor activities.

▪ Edit Modes

In Session 4, you learned how to use the basic tools for word processor activities. Every time you use the computer to work with a word processor file, you will be using these tools again and again. Now is a good time to review the things you learned in Session 4.

Creating a word processor file   There must be a word processor file on the Desktop before you can use the word processor program in AppleWorks. Often you will want to work with a file that already exists on your Computer Applications DATA Disk. In that case, you simply move the file from the disk to the Desktop. Or, you may want to make an empty file to hold new text. In either case, you use the Add files command on the Main Menu. The computer then guides you through the steps for putting a word processor file on the Desktop.

Text insert mode   When you first reach the REVIEW/ADD/ CHANGE screen, AppleWorks places you in **insert mode**. This means that letters or characters that you type at the keyboard go into the file at the position of the cursor. Any letters to the right of the cursor move over to make room for the new text. In insert mode, the cursor is a flashing underline symbol.

Exchange mode   There is another mode that you did not see in the hands-on session. This is called the **exchange mode**. In the exchange mode, each letter you type replaces the letter at the cursor position. The cursor moves forward in the file as the exchange process goes on. In the exchange mode, the cursor is a flashing rectangle of light.

Changing modes   The Edit command (⌂ E) acts like an on-off (toggle) switch. If you are in the insert mode, the (⌂ E) command switches to the exchange mode. If you are in the exchange mode, the (⌂ E) command switches to the insert mode.

Which mode is best?   The exchange mode is useful for certain tasks, such as capitalizing a word that was written in lowercase. However, accidents cause more damage in the exchange mode than in the insert mode. If you tap a key by accident in the exchange mode, you erase part of the file. This does not happen in the insert mode. Instead, the accidental letter is inserted in the file and can be deleted easily. To avoid accidents, we use the insert mode throughout this book.

▪ Editing Word Processor Files

Usually, when you review a paper you have written, you see many ways to make improvements. Perhaps there are spelling errors. Perhaps you think of a word that would be better than one in the text. Or perhaps whole phrases or sentences should be replaced. If you are working with paper and pencil, you may have to rewrite the complete paper several times. This takes time and effort. You may be tempted to leave the paper as is, even when you know how to improve it.

Word processor editing The situation is quite different when you are using a word processor program. Since changes are easy to make, you will probably want to make them. You can work through a file as many times as you need to make your improvements. No painful rewriting or retyping is needed. When you are happy with the result, you can have the computer print a clean copy.

Deleting text All editing has two parts: deleting old text and inserting new material. As you saw in Session 4, the (DELETE) key removes characters from a file. Each time you tap the key, the character to the left of the cursor is removed. (If the cursor is at the beginning of a line, it moves to the end of the previous line.) You can remove many characters quickly by holding the (DELETE) key down. You can remove several complete lines this way if you wish. (In Session 6, you will learn a better way to delete large blocks of text.)

Inserting text As soon as you have deleted the old word or phrase, you are ready to insert the change. The cursor is at the correct place for you to begin typing. Simply type the new material on the keyboard. The computer inserts it at the proper place in the file. (If the computer should happen to be in the exchange mode, you will see the rectangular-shaped cursor. If so, use the (ᴓ E) command to go back to the insert mode before typing.)

Saving a file Once you have edited a file, you will want to save the new version. To do this, you must leave the REVIEW/ADD/CHANGE screen and go to the Main Menu. Then you give the Save Desktop command and follow directions when they appear on the screen. If the disk contains an old version of the file, the computer gives you two choices: You may either replace the old version with the new one or change the file name and save it with the new name. Normally, you want to replace the old with the new.

Printing a file After you are happy with all the changes you have made to your file, you will want a printed copy. You can get one if there is a printer connected to your computer or if you can take your disk to a computer that has a printer attached. First, you must put a copy of the file on the AppleWorks Desktop. Second, you must be at the REVIEW/ADD/CHANGE screen with the file visible. Then you must carry out these steps:

1. Make sure the printer is connected, turned on, and ready to receive information from the computer.
2. Give the Print command (⌘ P).
3. If prompted, put your AppleWorks Program Disk in the drive. Then tap (RETURN).
4. Tap (RETURN) to print the whole file.
5. Select the name of the printer you are using and then tap (RETURN).
6. Tap (RETURN) to print one copy of the file.

The key step to remember is the (⌘ P) command. The computer prompts you for the rest of the steps. All you have to do is read the messages on the screen and follow instructions.

▪ The Basics of Word Processing

There is a great deal you have not yet learned about the word processor program in AppleWorks. Nevertheless, the skills you have learned here are fundamental. No matter which word processor program you use, you will be doing the same things over and over.

Loading a document   There is a variety of ways by which text information can be loaded into the computer and made available to the word processor program. In Session 4, you created a new file and typed the information at the keyboard. In Session 6, you will move several word processor files from disk into the computer's memory. It is even possible to have your computer receive a file sent by another computer and store it on disk. From there, you can move the file into the computer's memory. From whatever source, the document must be in the computer's memory before you can use the editing tools.

Editing a document   The simplest **editing** tools are often the most useful. Different word processors each have their own ways to carry out editing operations. Some are dazzling in the way they work or in their efficiency. In the end, however, all use the same processes you have learned about in Sessions 4 and 5. To edit a document, you must first locate the text passage that is to be changed. Then the material to be changed is deleted from the file. In AppleWorks, you used the (DELETE) key to do this. Finally, if new material is to be inserted, it is typed at the keyboard. You found that this was especially easy in AppleWorks since the computer is usually in the insert mode. No matter how complicated the document is or how many changes must be made, each step in the editing process is done using these three operations.

Printing a document   A word processor file is stored in magnetic form on a disk. Almost always though, you will want a **hard copy** of the document, that is, a copy printed on paper. To get a hard copy, you must have a printer connected to your computer. Each word processor program has built-in commands that tell the computer how to do this. In AppleWorks, you use the (⌂ P) command to tell the computer you want to send information to the printer.

QUESTIONS

1. At what screen must you be to insert or delete text in a word processor file?
2. What command do you use to toggle between the insert mode and the exchange mode?
3. How can you tell whether the computer is in the insert mode or the exchange mode?
4. What does wordwrap mean?
5. What is the main reason why word processor editing is easier than paper-and-pencil methods?
6. In AppleWorks, how do you delete a word from a file?
7. In AppleWorks, how do you insert a word at a particular place in a file?
8. Suppose you try to save file MyText and your disk already contains a file with this name. What two choices does the computer give you?
9. In AppleWorks, where must a file be before it can be sent to the printer?
10. In AppleWorks, what command tells the computer you want to send a file to the printer?
11. At what screen must you be to start the process of sending a file to the printer?

6 More Word Processor Tools

SESSION GOALS:
- Scroll the text of a long file up and down the screen.
- Use keyboard commands to move the cursor quickly to any part of a file.
- Use keyboard commands to find pieces of text and to replace old text with new text.
- Use keyboard commands to move, copy, and delete whole blocks of text.
- Save a Desktop file with a new name.

▪ Starting the Computer

So far, you have seen only small pieces of text on the REVIEW/ADD/CHANGE screen. In this session, you will see how the word processor program handles files that are too big to fit on the screen.

Start the computer with AppleWorks in the usual way.

If you need a reminder about how to do this, see page 32.

Give the `Add files` command from the Main Menu.

Give the `current disk` command from the Add Files menu.

If prompted, follow the instructions for swapping disks.

After you insert your Computer Applications DATA Disk and tap
(RETURN), your screen should look similar to the figure on the next page.

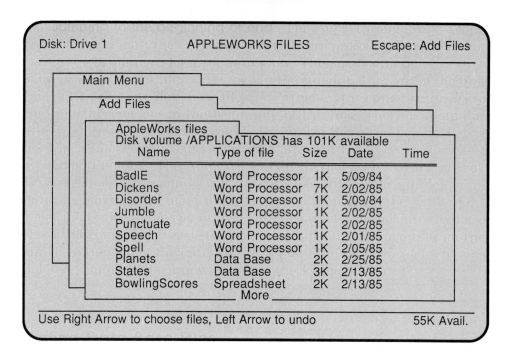

Disk: Drive 1   APPLEWORKS FILES   Escape: Add Files

```
Main Menu
  Add Files
    AppleWorks files
    Disk volume /APPLICATIONS has 101K available
      Name          Type of file    Size    Date      Time
      BadIE         Word Processor   1K     5/09/84
      Dickens       Word Processor   7K     2/02/85
      Disorder      Word Processor   1K     5/09/84
      Jumble        Word Processor   1K     2/02/85
      Punctuate     Word Processor   1K     2/02/85
      Speech        Word Processor   1K     2/01/85
      Spell         Word Processor   1K     2/05/85
      Planets       Data Base        2K     2/25/85
      States        Data Base        3K     2/13/85
      BowlingScores Spreadsheet      2K     2/13/85
                         More
```

Use Right Arrow to choose files, Left Arrow to undo   55K Avail.

You are looking at the directory of your Computer Applications DATA Disk. Notice the size of the files. Most are 1K in length. This means that they each contain 1024 characters at most. File Dickens, however, is a 7K file. This is the one you will explore now.

Use the ↓ key to select Dickens. Then tap RETURN.

If prompted, insert the AppleWorks Program disk and tap RETURN.

1. What is the purpose of the AppleWorks Files menu?
2. What does 7K tell you about file Dickens?

▪ Scrolling the Text

You should now be at the REVIEW/ADD/CHANGE screen. At the upper left, you should see the file name Dickens. The text of this file is too long to fit on one screen.

Use the ↓ key to move the cursor to line 20. (The cursor location is given at the bottom of the screen.)

Tap the ↓ key twice more.

Two lines disappear at the top of the screen and two new lines appear at the bottom. This is called **scrolling**. Notice that the cursor is now at line 22 of the file.

Hold the ⬇ **key down for a few seconds.**

You should see the text of the file scroll rapidly up the screen.

Hold the ⬇ **key down until scrolling stops.**

The cursor is now at line 114 of file Dickens. You are looking at the text at the end of the file.

3. What does scrolling mean?
4. What key can you use to cause the text to scroll toward the end of the file?

■ Making Big Cursor Moves

You could use the ⬆ key in the same way to get back to the beginning of the file. But there is a faster way.

Hold down the ⓒ **key and tap** ①.

In the future, such key combinations will be printed like this: ⓒ①. The ⓒ① command tells the computer to move the cursor to the beginning of the file.

Give the command ⓒ⑨.

That tells the computer to move the cursor to the end of the file.

Give the command ⓒ⑤.

That places the cursor at line 57, the middle line in the file. You can use other number keys with ⓒ to move quickly to other parts of the file. There is another way to move the cursor rapidly through the file.

Give the ⓒ① **command to move the cursor to the beginning of the file.**

Give the command ⓒ⬇.

That command moves the cursor to the bottom line of whatever text is on the screen.

Give the ⓒ⬇ **command again.**

When the cursor is already on the bottom line of the screen, this same command has a different effect. The effect is to display the next 20 lines (one full screen) of text.

Keep giving the (⌂|↓) **command until the cursor is at the end of the file.**

Give the command (⌂|↑).

As you might guess, the (⌂|↑) command works like the (⌂|↓) command. If the cursor is not at the top of the screen, the (⌂|↑) command moves it to the top line.

Give the (⌂|↑) **command again.**

If the cursor is already at the top line on the screen, the (⌂|↑) command moves the cursor 20 lines (one full screen) up in the file.

Keep giving the (⌂|↑) **command until the cursor is at the beginning of the file.**

5. What command moves the cursor to the beginning of the file?
6. What does the (⌂|↓) command do if the cursor is in the middle of the screen?
7. What does the (⌂|↓) command do if the cursor is at the bottom of the screen?

▪ Moving the Cursor a Word at a Time

You have seen how to move up and down through a file quickly. You can also move the cursor left and right quickly.

Move the cursor to the beginning of line 8.

Tap (→) **until the cursor is at the beginning of the word** times.

This method works, but it is slow. Try a faster way.

Give the (⌂|→) **command.**

This command moves the cursor forward one whole word at a time.

Give the (⌂|←) **command.**

That moves the cursor back one word. The (⌂) commands with arrow keys let you move the cursor rapidly through the file. You can move left or right one word at a time. You can move up or down one screen at a time.

8. What does the (⌂|→) command do?
9. What is the difference between using an arrow key by itself and using the same arrow key with the (⌂) key?

▪ Finding Text

Often, you want to move the cursor to a word that you know is somewhere in the file, but you do not know where. AppleWorks has a command to find text.

Move the cursor to the beginning of the file.

Give the command (ᵼ)(F).

The top line shows that you are at the Find screen. (As usual, tapping (ESC) will undo the command.) The bottom line is prompting you for input.

Use the (→) and (←) arrow keys to select each of the different options. Do *not* tap (RETURN) yet.

There are five kinds of things you can find: Text, Page, Marker, Case sensitive text, and Options for printer. You will be looking for Text.

Select Text and tap (RETURN).

The prompt at the bottom of the screen asks you to enter whatever text you want the computer to find.

Type king and tap (RETURN).

The line containing king is now in the middle of the screen, and the word is highlighted. The prompt at the bottom of the screen asks if you want to find the next occurrence of the word. No is already selected. If you found the word you are looking for, you can quit by either tapping (RETURN) or (N). If you are looking for another occurrence of the word, you tap (Y).

Tap (Y) to find the next occurrence of king.

This is the second occurrence of the word.

Tap (Y) again.

As you see, the computer found king, but it is a part of another word. The important point to remember is that the computer searches for a series of letters. It highlights that series whenever it finds it, whether as a separate word, a part of a word, or a whole group of words.

Tap (Y) again.

This time, the computer found king inside the word taking.

Tap (Y) once more.

The beep and the prompt at the bottom of the screen tell you that the computer did not find any more occurrences.

As directed, tap the spacebar to get back to the REVIEW/ADD/CHANGE screen.

Move the cursor to the beginning of the file. Give the ⌒ F command, select Text, **and tap** RETURN .

The computer remembers the last word you wanted to find. If you wanted to look for king again, you would just tap RETURN . To look for a different word, say queen, you must first delete the word already there.

Give the Yank command ⌒ Y .

This tells the computer to "yank out" all characters from the cursor to the end of the line.

Type queen **and tap** RETURN .

Tap Y **to continue the search.**

The computer found the word queen once more.

Tap N **to stop the search.**

10. What command moves the cursor to a word or phrase that you type on the keyboard?
11. What command erases characters from the cursor to the end of the line?

▪ Finding and Replacing Text

Quite often, the reason you want to find a word is to change it to another word. AppleWorks has a single command for finding one piece of text and replacing it with new text.

Here is an example. The Dickens passage uses British spelling for English words. American spelling is usually the same but not always. For example, Dickens uses the word "gaol" where an American would write "jail." You can use a word processor to replace "gaol" with "jail" everywhere in the file.

Move the cursor to the beginning of the file.

Give the Replace command ⌒ R .

In this mode, the computer will look for only two things: Text or Case sensitive text. **Case sensitive** means that the computer should treat uppercase and lowercase versions of the same letter as different characters. For example, "Gaol" and "gaol" are treated differently. In Text mode, however, capitalization should be ignored when searching for a word or phrase.

Select Case sensitive text **and tap** (RETURN).

This is the safest choice when replacing text, since you usually do not want to replace a capitalized word with one that is not capitalized.

The prompt at the bottom of the screen is asking for the text that you want the computer to find. If there is text there already, you should erase it.

Give the Yank command (⌘ Y).

Type the word gaol **and tap** (RETURN).

The new prompt asks for the replacement word.

Type the word jail **and tap** (RETURN).

The next prompt asks if you want to replace the words one at a time or all the words in the file at the same time. It is safer to replace words one at a time. That allows you to check each change before the computer makes it.

Select One at a time **and tap** (RETURN).

As you can see, the computer found gaol in the word gaols. The prompt at the bottom of the screen asks whether you want to replace this one or not.

Tap (Y).

Now the old spelling is gone. The new spelling has replaced it. The next step is to see if there are any more occurrences of gaol in the file.

Tap (Y) **to find the next occurrence.**

The computer did not find any.

Tap the spacebar to get back to the REVIEW/ADD/CHANGE screen.

That completes the replacement process. You can use the same process to change the British spelling of "recognise" to the American spelling "recognize."

Move the cursor to the beginning of the file.

Use the (⌘ R) **command to replace** ise **with** ize, **one at a time.**

You should have found only one occurrence of the British spelling.

Tap the spacebar to go back to the REVIEW/ADD/CHANGE screen.

As we said earlier, it is possible to have the computer make all the replacements without asking you about each one. This is a powerful command, but you have to be very careful when you use it. On the next page is an example of how things can go wrong.

Move the cursor to the beginning of the file.

Give the ⌘ R command. Select Case sensitive text **and tap** RETURN.

At the prompt, erase ise, **type** we, **and tap** RETURN.

At the next prompt, erase ize, **type** the people, **and tap** RETURN.

At the final prompt, select All **and tap** RETURN.

Notice the text near the cursor. It reads musketeers the peoplent into St. Giles's.

Move the cursor to line 70, column 41.

The text near the cursor reads they the peoplere awake. You probably see the problem. You replaced we by the people wherever we appeared. This was done even when the letters we were buried inside other words, such as went and were. One way to avoid problems like this is to type a space before and after the word you are searching for. Also, type a space before and after the replacement word.

Suppose you make a serious mistake while using the Replace command. What can be done? One solution is to work your way through the file and repair all damage. Sometimes it is easier to throw away all your changes and begin with a fresh copy of the file. Let us do that now.

Go back to the Main Menu. Give the Remove files **command.**

If necessary, select the file name Dickens **and then tap** RETURN.

Give the command Throw out the changes to a file.

Tap Y **to tell the computer you really do want to throw away the file containing the changes.**

At this point, the copy of Dickens that was on the Desktop is gone. However, the original version is still on your Computer Applications DATA Disk. If you wanted to make further changes, you could place a fresh copy of the file onto the Desktop.

12. What command replaces one phrase you type with another phrase you type?
13. What is the safest way to replace one word with another everywhere in the file?

▪ Moving Text

When writing, you often need to do more than just correct spelling or change a few words. You might want to change the order of phrases in a sentence, move sentences around in a paragraph, or move whole paragraphs.

With only pencil and paper, you would have to rewrite whole pages. With a word processor program, however, you can easily move any block of text from one place to another.

Duplicate a copy of file Jumble **from your Computer Applications DATA Disk to the Desktop.**

Read the paragraph. Think about how it could be improved.

You probably had trouble following what the writer had in mind. What does "It is" in the first sentence refer to? Why is the second sentence not closer to the fifth sentence, which also talks about saving files?

By itself, each sentence contains useful information. However, the reader does not get the sense of the paragraph until the very end. In fact, the last sentence is really the topic sentence. It should go first. You can move it there easily.

Move the cursor under the letter T **at the beginning of the last sentence.**

Give the Move command (⌘ M).

This command gives you the Move Text screen. You see a new prompt and three options at the bottom of the screen.

Give the Within document **command by tapping** (RETURN).

There are three changes on the screen. First, the computer now shows the places in the text where the (RETURN) key was tapped. These places are marked by a checkerboard character that we will call a blob. Second, the letter at the cursor position is now highlighted. Finally, there is a new prompt at the bottom of the screen.

Use the arrow keys to highlight the last sentence, including the period and the two spaces after it, but not the blob.

Now you have selected the sentence. Here is how to move it.

Tap (RETURN).

The sentence is still selected, but there is a new prompt.

Move the cursor under the I **at the beginning of the paragraph. Then tap** (RETURN).

That did it. The computer moved the selected text to the new cursor location. Take a moment to read the paragraph again. It makes more sense now but still could be improved. The first two sentences go together nicely, but the third sentence belongs at the end.

Put the cursor under the S **at the beginning of the third sentence.**

Use the ⌧ M command and the arrow keys to select the whole sentence, including the period and spaces that follow it. Then tap RETURN.

Move the cursor under the final blob. Then tap RETURN.

Once again, the computer moves the selected text to the new cursor position. You can use this method to move any selected text (words, phrases, sentences, paragraphs, etc.) to a new location in the file.

Once in a while, you may want to make a duplicate copy of some of the text in a file. Or, you may want to delete a large block of text. There are AppleWorks commands for doing both these things. First, let us make a duplicate copy of the whole paragraph.

Move the cursor to the beginning of the paragraph. Give the Copy command ⌧ C.

You are now at the Copy Text screen. The prompt line is exactly the same as on the Move Text screen. As before, you want the copy to be within the same **document**. (AppleWorks sometimes refers to files as documents.)

Tap RETURN.

Use the ↓ key to select the complete paragraph. Tap RETURN.

Move the cursor down several lines. Tap RETURN.

Now you can see both the original paragraph and the duplicate copy. Deleting a block of text is even simpler. As an exercise, here is how to delete the top copy of the paragraph.

Move the cursor to the beginning of the top paragraph. Give the Delete command ⌧ D.

You are at the Delete Text screen.

Use the ↓ key to select the whole paragraph and any blank lines following it. Tap RETURN.

That is all there is to it.

14. What command moves a block of text from one place to another in the file?
15. What command makes a duplicate copy of a block of text?
16. What command erases a block of text?

▪ Saving a File with a Different Name

Sometimes when working with a file on the Desktop, you want to save the changed version but not destroy the original version on the disk. That turns out to be easy to do.

Go back to the Main Menu and give the `Save Desktop` **command.**

Tap `RETURN` **to save file** `Jumble`.

At the next menu, give the `current disk` **command.**

The menu does not change this time, but the text on the menu does. The computer warns you that file `Jumble` is already on your disk. You can either replace the old copy with the changed version or save the changed version with a different name. You want the second option.

Give the `different name` **command.**

At the new prompt, give the Yank command to delete the file name `Jumble`. **Type the name** `Organized` **and tap** `RETURN`.

You have now done what you set out to do. The disk drive light came on while the computer wrote the new version into the file named `Organized`.

Tap `ESC` **to go back to the REVIEW/ADD/CHANGE screen.**

Look at the upper left corner of the screen.

The information there shows that the name of the file on the Desktop has also been changed from `Jumble` to `Organized`.

That brings you to the end of these activities. If you have time, do some of the On Your Own activities. Then quit the computer in the usual way.

17. Why might you want to change the name of a file before saving it?

18. How can you change the name of a file before saving it?

If you have time:

ON YOUR OWN

- Clear the Desktop. Put file `Dickens` back on the Desktop. Practice cursor moves. Practice finding words and phrases. Practice replacing words. Practice moving, copying, and deleting blocks of text.
- Clear the Desktop. Put file `Disorder` on the Desktop. This file needs to be put in alphabetical order. Use the Move command to alphabetize the list of file names. Change the file name to `Order` and save it.
- Clear the Desktop. Put file `BadIE` on the Desktop. The words in this file do not follow the *i* before *e* spelling rule. Use the Replace command to change `ei` to `ie` as needed. Use the replace command again to change `ie` to `ei` as needed. Change the file name to `GoodIE` and save it.

7 Using the Word Processor

SESSION GOALS: • Review different ways to move the cursor through a file.
• Review the steps for finding and replacing text in a word processor file.
• Review commands for deleting, moving, and copying blocks of text.
• Understand the need to save a file often while editing it.
• Understand the impact of word processing on writing.

▪ Moving through a Large File

In Session 6, you learned more about using a word processor to help with writing tasks. This time, you worked with a much larger file than the one you wrote in Session 4.

The Dickens file The text in file Dickens was 114 lines long—nearly six times as much as you can see at one time on the computer screen. The arrow keys give you a simple way to move from letter to letter or line to line in the file. However, with only the arrow keys, it would take a long time to move from the beginning to the end of a big file. All word processor programs give you other commands for moving quickly through a file.

Scrolling up and down In AppleWorks, when you hold any key down, the effect is the same as if you had tapped the key again and again. One fairly quick way to move down the lines of a file is to hold the ⬇ key down. The cursor quickly goes the bottom line on the screen. After that, the cursor stays at the bottom of the screen, but the text in the file starts moving up the screen. As each new line appears at the bottom, a line disappears at the top. This is called *scrolling*; the text moves up the screen as if it were written on a scroll of paper that someone was rolling up behind the screen.

Jumping to the beginning or end Many times when working on a file, you want to jump quickly to the beginning or the end. The keyboard command ⌂1 puts the first 20 lines of the file on the screen. The command ⌂9 brings the end of the file into view.

Jumping to the middle In the same way, the command ⌂5 brings the middle of the file into view. The middle line of the file appears at the middle of the screen. The cursor is at the beginning of the line. Other number keys used with the ⌂ key cause jumps to other lines. Think of the file as being divided into eight parts. ⌂1 moves the cursor to the top line of the first part. $\boxed{\texttt{ɔ}\,|\,2}$ moves to the top line of the second part. $\boxed{\texttt{ɔ}\,|\,3}$ moves to the top line of the third part, and so on.

Moving by screens The AppleWorks REVIEW/ADD/CHANGE screen shows 20 lines of a word processor file at a time. The command $\boxed{\texttt{ɔ}\,|\,\downarrow}$ allows you to move through the file one full screen at a time. If the cursor is not already at the bottom screen line, this command will put it there. After that, each $\boxed{\texttt{ɔ}\,|\,\downarrow}$ brings another 20 lines of the file into view. In this way, you can quickly go through an entire file without missing any lines. In the same way, the $\boxed{\texttt{ɔ}\,|\,\uparrow}$ command allows you to move backward through the file, one full screen at a time.

Moving by words You should think of the $\boxed{\texttt{ɔ}}$ key as a magnifier for the arrow keys. The $\boxed{\uparrow}$ key moves the cursor up one line. The $\boxed{\texttt{ɔ}\,|\,\uparrow}$ command moves the cursor up many lines. The $\boxed{\texttt{ɔ}}$ key has a similar effect on the left and right arrow keys. The command $\boxed{\texttt{ɔ}\,|\,\rightarrow}$ moves the cursor to the beginning of the next word in the file. $\boxed{\texttt{ɔ}\,|\,\leftarrow}$ moves the cursor to the beginning of the previous word. Holding down both $\boxed{\texttt{ɔ}}$ and $\boxed{\rightarrow}$ is like giving the $\boxed{\texttt{ɔ}\,|\,\rightarrow}$ command again and again. This is a handy way to move the cursor quickly through a sentence or paragraph.

Finding and Replacing Text

Sometimes when working with a word processor program, you remember a word or phrase that is somewhere in the file—but you cannot recall where. Nearly all word processor programs have a command for finding text and bringing it into view. This command is often called the **search** command. In AppleWorks it is called the Find or $\boxed{\texttt{ɔ}\,|\,\texttt{F}}$ command. Here are the steps you use to find the word king in the Dickens file.

1. Move the cursor to the beginning of the file.
2. Give the Find command $\boxed{\texttt{ɔ}\,|\,\texttt{F}}$.
3. Select the Text option and tap $\boxed{\text{RETURN}}$.
4. Enter the word to be found (king). You may have to erase a word or phrase already there before entering your word.
5. The computer finds the word and shows the part of the file containing it. If you want to find the next occurrence of the word, tap $\boxed{\text{Y}}$. Otherwise, tap $\boxed{\text{N}}$.

The important things to remember are the first two steps. After that, the computer prompts you for more information.

Finding parts of words When you asked the computer to search for king, it found the word "king" twice, but it also found the same four letters as parts of the words "making" and "taking." The computer looks for any match it can find between the text you type and the text in the file.

Case sensitive text Sometimes, you want to find a word whether or not it is capitalized. At other times, capitalization matters: If you type KING, you do *not* want the computer to find king. Like most other word processor programs, AppleWorks lets you say what kind of search you want. If you select Text at step 3 above, the computer ignores capitalization. If you select Case sensitive text, the computer pays attention to capitalization. In other words, the computer is sensitive to whether each letter is an uppercase or a lowercase letter.

Erasing the previous selection If you use the (ᵹ F) command a second time, the computer remembers the last word or phrase you were looking for. When it comes time for you to enter new text, you must first erase the old text. The simplest way to do this is to use the Yank command (ᵹ Y). It tells the computer to erase all text from the cursor to the end of the line. You can also use this command when the cursor is on a line of the word processor file. It has the same effect there.

Replacing text Most word processor programs have a powerful (and sometimes dangerous) command called search and replace. Suppose that you have written a report on Buffalo Bill. Later, you discover that you misspelled his name as Bufalo. Here is how to use the AppleWorks Replace command to fix all the misspellings in the whole file:

1. Move the cursor to the beginning of the file.
2. Give the Replace command (ᵹ R).
3. Choose Case sensitive text and tap (RETURN).
4. Enter the word you want to find (Bufalo).
5. Enter the word you want to replace it with (Buffalo).
6. Select All (not One at a time) and tap (RETURN).

Again, the important things to remember are the first two steps. The computer prompts you after that. As soon as you carry out the last step, the computer begins searching the file. Whenever it finds the old text, it replaces it with the new text.

Using abbreviations The Replace command can make life easy when you are writing a paper that contains the same phrase again and again. For example, if you were writing about the United States and the Soviet Union, you could just type US and SU as quick abbreviations. When the paper was finished, you could use the Replace command to change US to United States everywhere. Then you could change SU to Soviet Union.

▪ Things to Watch Out For

You must be very careful when you tell the computer to replace *all* occurrences of one piece of text with another piece of text. For example, suppose that you used USSR in the same paper that contained your US abbreviation. The Replace command in the previous paragraph would change USSR to United StatesSR everywhere in the file.

Playing it safe To avoid accidents, the safest approach when using the (ó|R) command is to change step 6 to Select One at a time instead of All. Then, the computer stops and asks whether you want each change made. If you say yes, the computer makes the change and keeps searching. If you say no, the change is not made and the search stops. (You can restart it with another (ó|R) command.)

Disaster time No matter how careful you are, sooner or later you will make a mistake while editing. In trying to fix the first error, you may find things getting worse and worse. What should you do? Probably, the best course is to erase the version of the file in the computer's memory. (In AppleWorks terms, remove it from the Desktop.) Then put the last version you saved on your disk back into memory.

Strong advice What if you have not saved a copy on your disk? Then you are out of luck. You have much typing and editing ahead. You can be ready for such disasters if you follow this simple advice: Every 10 minutes or so, save your work on the disk. In AppleWorks, there is a quick way to do this: Give the Save command (ó|S) directly from the REVIEW/ADD/CHANGE screen. If disaster strikes later, you have lost only a few minutes of work.

▪ Editing Blocks of Text

You can do any editing job if you can find a word, delete it, and insert a new word. For some jobs, however, these simple methods can take a long time and a lot of typing. For example, you could move one paragraph ahead of another one by first deleting the second paragraph, a character at a time. Then, you could insert the same paragraph, a character at a time, at the new location. Most word processors have special commands for doing things like this. These commands work on whole blocks of text.

Deleting a block The simplest block-editing tool is the Delete command (ó|D). To use it, you first place the cursor at the first character of the block of text you want to delete. Next, you give the command. When prompted, you use any cursor-moving commands to select the text you wish to delete. As you select the text, the computer highlights it on the screen. After you select the block, you tap (RETURN) to delete it.

Another warning If you change your mind before tapping (RETURN), you can back out of the Delete command by tapping (ESC). Once you tap (RETURN), however, the text is removed from the copy of the file on the

Desktop. There are only two ways to get it back: retype it (if you remember what it was) or get a fresh copy of the file from your disk. This is another reason to save a copy of the file you are working on every few minutes.

Moving a block The Move command (⌘ M) works a lot like the Delete command. You first select the block of text you want moved. Then you tap (RETURN). The text disappears, as before. This time, however, the text is not lost. The computer prompts you to put the cursor where you want the block to be inserted. After you put the cursor there and tap (RETURN), the computer inserts the entire block automatically.

Copying a block The Copy command (⌘ C) works exactly like the Move command, with one exception. The block you select is not deleted from the file. The result after the insertion is that you have two identical blocks of text in the file.

▪ Impact of Word Processor Programs

In Part B, you learned to use the AppleWorks word processor program as an aid to writing and editing. Other word processors have different commands, but they all do the same basic things. These programs are making fundamental changes in the way people do writing tasks.

The typing pool Working in any kind of office is working with information. In the past, most office information began on paper. A manager would use pen or pencil to write a draft of a letter, a memo, or a report. Or else, a secretary would take dictation in a shorthand notebook. Then the information would be sent to the **typing pool**—a group of people whose only job was to read words on paper and type them on a typewriter. The typed versions would go back to the authors for more editing, then back to the typing pool for retyping, then back to the authors for review.

The electronic office In a modern office, things work differently. There is no need for anyone to begin with pencil and paper. Instead, the writer of a letter or report enters the first draft at a computer with a word processor program. The draft appears on the screen, and the author edits the text immediately. When satisfied with the content, the author saves the file on a disk and gives instructions, usually by computer, to have the file printed automatically. In a few minutes, the author has a finished copy. No retyping is necessary.

The paperless office If a business has computers in all offices, it can often eliminate the final step: the typed copy. A person who wants to send a memo to someone in another office can send the file electronically to a central computer. The computer can be in the same building or can be thousands of miles away. The person who is to receive the memo will get it electronically from the central computer and read it on a screen.

Old skills When office information systems were based solely on paper documents, certain skills were very important. There was much demand for high-speed typists who could type a whole page without a mistake. Secretaries needed to know how to take dictation in shorthand. They also needed to know how to maintain file drawers crammed with information on paper.

New skills Computers and word processor programs are making rapid changes in the skills needed to work in a modern office. Today, information can be created at personal computers or terminals. Both managers and clerical workers need good keyboard skills. However, speed and accuracy are far less important, since word processor files need be typed only once and are easy to edit. All office workers also need new skills for working with information stored in computer files, not just file drawers.

Computer literacy If you develop an understanding of computers and the way they work, you will have made a good start in preparing for work in a modern office. If you know how to enter information into a computer file, how to edit it, how to save a copy on a disk, and how to print a file, you already have important skills for the future. If you also understand computer concepts, such as input, processing, output, memory, and the role of computer programs, you will be better able to adapt to the changes brought about by the computer. In short, computer literacy is the basic skill needed.

Writing for pleasure Apart from work, people also write for pleasure. As you learn to use a word processor program, you will probably find much more satisfaction using it than using paper-and-pencil (and eraser!) methods. You can begin by typing your thoughts as they come, not worrying about how the finished letter or report will look. You can easily erase errors, insert new ideas in the middle, delete parts, and move whole paragraphs from place to place. Many people discover that this freedom changes writing from a burdensome job into a pleasant activity.

QUESTIONS

1. What AppleWorks screen allows you to edit a file?
2. How many lines of a long word processor file are visible at one time when you are editing the file?
3. What does scrolling mean?
4. What command moves the cursor down through a file one full screen at a time?

5. What command moves the cursor to the last line of a file?

6. What command moves the cursor to the beginning of the next word in a word processor file?

7. Suppose you want to find the first occurrence of `king` in a file. What are the first two things you should do?

8. Suppose you want to replace `king` with `ruler` everywhere in a word processor file. What are the first two things you should do?

9. Suppose you want to find the first occurrence of `Queen` in a file. But you do not want the computer to find `queen`. When prompted, which should you choose: `Text` or `Case sensitive text`?

10. Why is it dangerous to use the `All` option with the `Replace` command?

11. What is the safest way to replace one word with another word everywhere in a file?

12. What are two ways to delete a paragraph from a word processor file?

13. Suppose you want to move a sentence from one place to another in a word processor file. What are the first two things you should do?

14. Suppose you want to make a copy of a block of five lines in a word processor file. What are the first two things you should do?

15. When you use the `Save Desktop` command, the computer asks whether you want to save the file with a `different name`. Why might you want to do this?

16. Why are typing speed and accuracy less important in a modern office than in an older office?

17. Why should both managers and clerks have good keyboard skills today?

▪ Keyboard Commands

(ⓒ C), **Copy**   Make a copy of a block of text and insert it in a new place in a word processor file.

(ⓒ D), **Delete**   Delete a text block from a word processor file.

(ⓒ E), **Edit mode**   Switch between exchange mode and insert mode.

(ⓒ F), **Find**   Find a word, phrase, or other series of characters in a word processor file. The search begins at the cursor position.

(ⓒ M), **Move**   Delete a block of text and insert it in a new place in a word processor file.

(ⓒ N), **Name**   Change the name of a file.

(ⓒ P), **Print**   Print a word processor file. This command also allows you to specify a format for the file.

(ⓒ R), **Replace**   Find a word, phrase, or other series of characters in a word processor file; then replace it with another series of characters. The search begins at the cursor position.

(ⓒ S), **Save**   Duplicate a copy of a file from the Desktop to the disk.

(ⓒ Y), **Yank**   Erase all characters from the cursor to the end of a text line.

(ⓒ 1), (ⓒ 9)   Move the cursor to the beginning or the end of a file.

(ⓒ 5),   Move the cursor to the middle of a file.

(ⓒ ↓), (ⓒ ↑)   Move the cursor down or up one screenful at a time.

(ⓒ ←), (ⓒ →)   Move the cursor left or right one word at a time.

▪ New Ideas

case sensitive   When searching for words or phrases in this mode, uppercase and lowercase letters are treated as different letters by the computer.

document   The same thing as a file.

edit   Add information to a file or delete information from it.

exchange mode   An editing mode. Typed characters take the place of those at the cursor position.

insert mode   An editing mode. Typed characters are inserted at the position of the cursor.

REVIEW/ADD/CHANGE screen   The screen upon which text is entered into an AppleWorks file, deleted from the file, or changed.

scroll   Move through a word processor file so that different parts become visible on the screen.

wordwrap   Automatic movement of a word to the next line when it is too long to fit on the current line.

Part C

The Data Base Program

In Part B, you learned to use a word processor program to help with the task of writing. Part C deals with the data base program in AppleWorks. It helps you with the task of getting useful information out of a large collection of data. Familiar examples of data bases are an address book, a card catalog in the library, an almanac, and a collection of baseball statistics.

Searching for information Using any data base means searching for whatever you want to know. Without a computer, the data is usually organized for only one kind of search. An address book is organized alphabetically by last name, since you usually use a friend's last name to locate his address. But what if you plan a trip to Chicago and you want to search your address book for the names of everyone who lives in Chicago? Or what if you have forgotten someone's last name but remember her first name; how can you find her address? These things are hard to do with an ordinary address book.

Computer data bases When a data base is in a computer system, searching is easy. With a single command, you can reorganize the data to suit your needs. For example, you could easily organize a computerized address book so all city names were in alphabetical order. That way, all Chicago dwellers would appear in a group in the list, and you could simply read them off. You could also quickly find everyone named Sarah or everyone who lived on Plum Street.

Similar commands Part C will show you how to search for information in a computer data base. You will learn a few new commands in these sessions. However, most of the commands you learned in Parts A and B also apply to data base files. There are a few small differences, but most of the old commands work the same way.

Exploring Data Bases

SESSION GOALS:
- Load a data base file into the computer's memory.
- Move the cursor through a data base file.
- Sort the records of a data base file.
- Change an entry in a data base file.
- Use a selection rule to get information from a data base.

▪ Loading a Data Base File

All the files you have worked with so far have been word processor files. Now it is time to explore a new application program—the **data base program**.

Start the computer with your AppleWorks disks as usual.

At the Main Menu, give the Add files **command.**

At the Add Files menu, give the current disk **command.**

If prompted, swap your Computer Applications DATA Disk for the AppleWorks Program Disk. Then tap (RETURN).

The AppleWorks Files menu shows you 10 file names at a time. You can see the rest by scrolling.

Use the (↑) **and** (↓) **keys to scroll up and down through the file directory.**

As you see, there are three types of files on the Computer Applications DATA Disk. The word processor files come first, and they are in alphabetical order. Next come the data base files, also in alphabetical order. Last come the spreadsheet files. Begin with a data base file.

Use the (↓) **key to select file** Planets. **Then tap** (RETURN).

Swap disks as directed.

```
File: Planets                REVIEW/ADD/CHANGE               Escape: Main Menu

Selection: All records


Planet Name    Diameter   Distance from Sun  Moons
===================================================================================
Mercury          3100         36.0              0
Venus            7519         67.2              0
Earth            7926         92.9              1
Mars             4218        141.5              2
Jupiter         88700        483.4             13
Saturn          75100        886.0             10
Uranus          29200       1782.0              5
Neptune         27700       2792.0              2
Pluto            3000       3675.0              1
_____
Type entry or use ᑕ commands                                    ᑕ-? for Help
```

As always, when you load a file into AppleWorks, the computer shows the contents of the file on the REVIEW/ADD/CHANGE screen. For a data base file, the REVIEW/ADD/CHANGE screen looks like a table. The words above the columns are headings for the table. The cursor is now at the first entry in the table.

1. What type of files are listed first on the AppleWorks disk directory?
2. How does the appearance of a data base file differ from that of a word processor file?

▪ Moving through the Table

Most of the things you learned about moving the cursor through a word processor file work the same way with data base files. However, there are a few differences.

Tap the (→) key six times.

That moves the cursor to the last letter of the first entry in the table.

Tap the (→) key two times more.

The beep tells you that the (→) key will not move the cursor from one entry in the table to the next.

Tap the (TAB) key.

As you see, the (TAB) key moves the cursor to the beginning of the next entry.

Tap the (←) key.

As before, the beep tells you that the (←) key will not move the cursor from one entry in the table to the previous one.

Give the command (ɔ | TAB).

That moves the cursor back to the beginning of the previous entry.

Tap the (TAB) key three times. Note where the cursor is. Tap (TAB) once more.

When the cursor is at the last entry in a row, the (TAB) key moves the cursor to the first entry in the next row. There are other ways to move from row to row.

Tap the (TAB) key. Now use the (↑) and (↓) keys to change rows.

Give the (ɔ | 1) command. Give the (ɔ | 9) command.

As usual, the (↑) and (↓) keys move the cursor vertically one row at a time. Also, the (ɔ | 1) and (ɔ | 9) commands move the cursor vertically to the first row and the last row in the table.

Give the (ɔ | 5) command.

The cursor is now at the middle line in the table. It looks as though the first four lines in the table are gone. This is not so.

Use the (↑) key to scroll to the top of the table.

As usual, scrolling brings other parts of a file into view.

3. How do you move the cursor to the next entry in a data base file? How do you move the cursor to the previous entry?

4. What are two ways to move the cursor to the top line of a file?

▪ Arranging the Table

You have learned all the important ways for moving the cursor through a data base file. These moves are important when you want to change an entry or to arrange the table differently.

Right now, the planets appear in the order of their distances from the sun. Mercury is closest, so it comes first. Pluto is farthest, so it comes last. You might want to view the table with the planet names in alphabetical order. Here is how you can **sort alphabetically**.

Put the cursor on any planet name. Give the Arrange command (ɔ | A).

You now see the Arrange (Sort) screen. The first menu item is From A to Z. This is alphabetical order, which is what we want.

Tap RETURN.

That is all there is to it. The rows in the tables have been rearranged so that the planet names are in alphabetical order. You can also put items in numerical order—that is, **sort numerically**.

Put the cursor on any planet diameter. Give the Arrange command.

Command three is from 0 to 9, which means increasing numerical order.

Give command 3 on the Arrange menu.

Now the table is arranged so that the smallest planet is first and the largest is last.

Arrange the table so that the planet with the largest number of moons is first.

The Arrange command (ᴓ A) lets you change the order of the rows in a data base file. This command makes it easy to find answers that would be difficult to get otherwise. You have been working with a very small data base file. The payoff when using these tools is far greater when the file contains hundreds of rows.

5. What command do you use to change the order of the rows in a data base file?

6. Where must the cursor be before you use the command referred to in question 5?

7. In a data base file you can sort the rows in alphabetical order. What are three other orders that you can specify?

▪ Changing Entries

Most useful data bases contain information that changes. Suppose an astronomer makes a more accurate measurement of the distance from the sun to Pluto. In that case, you would want to change that entry in your data base. Here is how to do that.

Move the cursor to the Distance from Sun entry for the planet Pluto.

If necessary, move the cursor to the beginning of the entry. Give the Yank command (ᴓ Y).

That erases all characters from the cursor to the end of the entry.

Read the top right corner of the screen. Tap ESC.

If you should happen to select the wrong entry and delete it, the (ESC) key lets you put it back.

Give the Yank command again. Type the number 3682.0.

You have made the change, but there is one more step.

Try to use the (TAB) **key to move to another entry. Try** (↑) **and** (↓).

Nothing works. You must first tell the computer whether to accept the new entry or restore the old entry.

Tap (RETURN).

Now the new entry is part of the file, and you can move the cursor at will.

Change the number of moons of Saturn from 10 **to** 12.

That completes your work with file Planets. You have seen how to move the cursor from an entry. You have rearranged the rows of the table into alphabetical and numerical order. Finally, you have seen how to change entries in the data base file.

8. If you want to change an entry in a data base file, what is the first step?

9. How do you delete an entry?

10. After you have typed a new entry, what must you do to make it become part of the data base?

▪ Practice with Another Data Base

To see the power of data base commands, you need a bigger file. Now is a good time to practice what you have learned.

Clear the file Planets **from the Desktop. When prompted, give the command for throwing out the changes you made.**

Add the file States **to the Desktop from your Computer Applications DATA Disk.**

You should now see part of file States on the REVIEW/ADD/ CHANGE screen. Each row contains seven pieces of data about one state. The entries are

1. The name of the state

2. The 1983 population

3. The area in square miles

4. The state capital

5. The average January temperature

6. The average July temperature

7. The year the state was admitted to the Union

Hold down the ⊥ key and scroll to the end of the file.

Scroll back to the beginning.

Practice using the TAB and ⌘ TAB keys to move from entry to entry.

The table is now arranged with state names in alphabetical order.

Arrange the table so that the capital names are in alphabetical order.

Arrange the table in order of area, with the largest state first.

If you did this correctly, Alaska should be at the top of the table, followed by Texas and California. If you do not have Alaska at the top, you probably used the wrong arrangement order. Any of the four possibilities is legal, but the results can be surprising. For example, you can "alphabetize" numbers. Let us see what happens if you do.

If necessary, put the cursor on an Area entry. Give the Arrange command ⌘ A. Finally, give the From A to Z command.

When you alphabetize numbers, all numbers that begin with 1 come ahead of all the numbers that begin with 2. That is why the number 10,577 comes before the number 2,057. You should always use alphabetical ordering with names and numerical ordering with numbers.

Use the Arrange command to find the state with the fifth largest area.

Find the state with the fourth coldest winter.

Find the first state to join the Union after the original 13 colonies.

The Arrange command is a very powerful tool you can use to organize information and answer questions about the data in a file. The larger the file, the more useful the Arrange command becomes.

11. How would you find the state with the fifth smallest population?

12. What method of sorting should not be used with a column containing numbers?

▪ Finding and Selecting Records

When working with the word processor program, you used the Find command ⌘ F to locate a word or phrase anywhere in a file. You can use this same command with a data base file, but it works a little differently. Here is how to find all the rows in the table that contain north.

Put the cursor at the beginning of the file.

Give the Find command ⌘ F.

You are at the Find Records screen. In a data base file, a **record** is the same thing as a row in the tables you have been looking at. The prompt at the bottom of the screen asks you to enter the characters you are looking for.

Type the characters north **and then tap** (RETURN).

The computer found two records that contained the characters north and displayed them. Note that the computer treats uppercase letters and lowercase letters the same when searching through the file.

Tap (ESC).

That puts you back at the REVIEW/ADD/CHANGE screen.

Use the Find command to locate the characters ana.

The computer found three records containing the characters ana. The second record contains ana twice.

Tap (ESC) **to get back to the REVIEW/ADD/CHANGE menu.**

Suppose you want to find all states that have an average July temperature of 72 degrees.

Use the Find command to locate the characters 72.

Whoops! The computer found five states, but only three of them were the ones you wanted. This is because the Find command searches *all* entries. The population of Texas contains the characters 72, so the computer selects the Texas record. Can you see why Hawaii was selected?

Tap (ESC).

The Find command lets you look for records containing a match with the characters you type. There is a more precise way to find records in a data base file.

Read the Selection **phrase near the top of the screen.**

This phrase tells you that currently all records in the data base file are selected. This means that you can see them all by scrolling. Here is how to select just the records for which the July temperature is 72 degrees.

Give the Record Selection command (ᣠ R).

A new Select Records screen appears. This screen shows a menu with the seven column headings.

Select Jul **and tap** (RETURN).

Now there are 12 possibilities on the menu. You want the first one.

Tap (RETURN) **to choose the first option.**

At the prompt, type the characters 72 **and tap** (RETURN). **Note the** Selection **phrase near the top of the screen.**

This phrase is an example of a **selection rule**. Later, you will see how to use the words and, or, and through to build more complex selection rules. For now, let us see what happens when you use this one.

Read the line at the top right of the screen. Then tap (ESC).

This time, the computer found only the three records you were looking for. It ignored 72 in all categories except July temperature.

Try to scroll up and down past the records in view.

You *are* back at the REVIEW/ADD/CHANGE screen now, but you are only looking at part of the data base file. You cannot just scroll to see the rest. However, there is a quick way to see the whole data base again.

Give the (ɔ̇ R) **command again. Read the prompt line. Then tap** (Y).

All records are now selected. This means that all records are either visible or can be reached by scrolling. Now, let us see a more interesting use of the (ɔ̇ R) command.

Give the (ɔ̇ R) **command. Select** Jan, **and tap** (RETURN).

Select is less than **and tap** (RETURN). **At the prompt, type** 32 **and tap** (RETURN).

The selection rule is Jan is less than 32. This means that you want to see all states with January temperatures less than 32 degrees.

Tap (ESC) **to see the records that satisfy the selection rule.**

Most states have an average winter temperature below freezing. Now let us look for states that are both cold in winter and hot in summer.

Give the (ɔ̇ R) **command. Tap** (RETURN) **at the prompt to select** No.

The old selection rule has disappeared, and the computer is waiting for a new rule.

Select Jan **and tap** (RETURN). **Select** is less than **and tap** (RETURN). **Type** 32 **and tap** (RETURN).

Now you have the same selection rule as before. This time, we will add another condition to the rule. We also want the Jul temperature to be greater than 72 degrees.

Tap (RETURN) **to add the word** and **to the selection rule.**

Select Jul **and tap** (RETURN). **Select** is greater than **and tap** (RETURN). **Finally, type** 72 **and tap** (RETURN).

Notice the new selection rule. At this point, the computer is waiting for you to add more phrases to the selection rule. However, nothing more is needed to find the states we are looking for.

Tap (ESC).

As you can see, the computer found 13 states with cold winters and hot summers. Let us look at a different kind of selection rule.

Give the (ɑ̇ R) command. Tap (RETURN) to begin the new selection rule.

The new selection rule will be to find all states admitted to the Union between 1850 and 1875.

Select Admitted and tap (RETURN). Then tap (RETURN) to add equals to the selection rule. Type 1850 and tap (RETURN).

Select through and tap (RETURN). Type 1875 and tap (RETURN).

The selection rule is now complete.

Tap (ESC).

The computer found seven states admitted to the Union between 1850 and 1875. By using the (ɑ̇ R) commands, you can set up many different kinds of selection rules. Whenever you work with a large data base, much of your time will be spent deciding on selection rules to pull the information you want out of the file.

That completes these guided activities in this session. If you have time, try some of the On Your Own activities. When you are finished, quit the computer in the usual way. Throw away the changes you have made to file States.

13. What does the phrase after the word Selection on the REVIEW/ADD/CHANGE screen tell you?

14. What command do you use to change the selection rule?

If you have time: **ON YOUR OWN**

- The file States should be on the Desktop. Make a selection rule to find all states with populations less than 1,000,000 *and* areas greater than 100,000. Change the rule to find all states either with populations less than 1,000,000 *or* with areas greater than 100,000. Notice the difference between "and" and "or" in these selection rules.

- The file States should be on the Desktop. Make a selection rule to find the states that are not too cold in the winter and not too hot in the summer. You decide which numbers to use in the selection rule.

Data Base Files

SESSION GOALS:
- Compare a data base file to a word processor file.
- Understand new terms for describing a data base file.
- Review the ways for moving the cursor through a data base file.
- Review the use of the Arrange command to sort records.
- Review the steps needed to build a new selection rule.

▪ The Parts of a Data Base File

In Session 8, you began using the data base program in AppleWorks. When you gave the `Add files` and `current disk` menu commands, the computer showed a directory containing the names of all files on your disk. By scrolling down through the directory, you saw three different types of files: word processor files, data base files, and spreadsheet files.

Similarities   In many ways, a data base file is similar to a word processor file. Both kinds of files contain information. You can scroll from beginning to end of either kind of file and see what it contains. You can insert and delete information in both. You can move blocks of information from place to place in both. You can make printed copies of both kinds of files. (When you learn about spreadsheet files, you will see that the same is true of them.)

Differences   The big difference between a word processor file and a data base file is the way the information in each file is organized. A word processor file contains only text. Text has a very simple organization: One character follows another, from the beginning of the file to the end. In a data base file, however, information is organized into groups of related items.

Appearance of data base files   When you select a data base file from the disk, the computer reads it into memory and shows you the file on the REVIEW/ADD/CHANGE screen. The figure on the next page shows how the file `Planets` looks when you first see it.

```
File: Planets              REVIEW/ADD/CHANGE              Escape: Main Menu

Selection: All records


Planet Name   Diameter   Distance from Sun  Moons
===================================================================================
Mercury          3100        36.0              0
Venus            7519        67.2              0
Earth            7926        92.9              1
Mars             4218       141.5              2
Jupiter         88700       483.4             13
Saturn          75100       886.0             10
Uranus          29200      1782.0              5
Neptune         27700      2792.0              2
Pluto            3000      3675.0              1




Type entry or use ⌂ commands                          ⌂-? for Help
```

Rows and columns The information in this data base file looks like a table. Each row has information about a single planet. All the data for Jupiter are in the fifth row. Each column has information of a single kind. The second column gives the diameters of all the planets. The headings above the table tell what kind of information is in each column.

Data base organization If you were a careful typist, you could create a table like this as a word processor file. Would it then become a data base? The answer is yes and no. It is yes, because the information would be organized like a data base. It is no, because you could not use the commands of the data base program to *reorganize* the information. The importance of a data base file comes from the fact that you can easily change the order of the rows or see only those rows that are of interest.

▪ Special Terms for Describing a Data Base

As you have seen, the basic organization of a data base file is like a table of rows and columns. Special terms are used to refer to the information in the table.

Entries The data at one place in the table is called an **entry**. For file `Planets`, the entry at the upper left corner of the table is `Mercury`. The entry at the bottom of column 3 is `3675.0`. You can think of a data base file as a collection of entries.

Records In the file `Planets`, all the information about a single planet is called a **record**. As you can see, a record in the file is the same as a row in the table shown on the REVIEW/ADD/CHANGE screen. There are nine records in the file `Planets`. Each record in this file contains four entries. Most data base files have many more records and many more entries per record.

Categories Each entry in a record belongs to a single **category**. (Many other data base programs refer to categories as **fields**.) A category describes information the data base file contains. In the file `Planets`, there are four categories: the planet name, the diameter, the distance from the sun, and the number of moons. The category names automatically appear as headings in the table shown on the REVIEW/ADD/CHANGE screen.

Summing up A data base file is a collection of *entries*. The entries are grouped into *records* (rows). Within a record, each entry falls into a separate *category* (column). When you give commands that reorganize a file, all the entries in one record stay together. Basically, working with a data base file means moving whole records from place to place.

▪ Moving the Cursor

As with a long word processor file, you can see only a few lines of a large data base file on the computer screen at a time. To work with a file, you need to move the cursor about on the screen. You also need to move hidden parts of the file into view. In Part B, you learned how to move about in a word processor file. Most AppleWorks cursor-movement commands work the same way with data base files. However, there are a few differences.

Arrow and Tab keys The ↑ and ↓ keys work exactly as before. To move back and forth through a single entry, you use the ← and → keys. However, you may *not* use these keys to move from entry to entry. Instead, the TAB key moves the cursor to the next entry, and ⌘ TAB moves it to the previous entry.

Open-Apple arrow keys The ⌘ ↑ and ⌘ ↓ commands work exactly as they did with word processor files. These commands allow you to move through a file one full screen at a time. (A word processor screen shows 20 lines of a file, whereas a data base screen shows 15 records.) However, the ⌘ ← and ⌘ → commands do not move the cursor through a data base file.

Jumping to the beginning or end   The $\boxed{\circ\ \uparrow}$ through $\boxed{\circ\ 9}$ commands work almost the same way as with word processor files. In either case, they bring parts of a file into view. The small difference is this: With word processor files, $\boxed{\circ\ \uparrow}$ moves the cursor to the *start* of the first line in the file; with data base files, $\boxed{\circ\ \uparrow}$ moves the cursor *vertically* to the first line but *not* to the beginning of the line. There is a similar difference in the way $\boxed{\circ\ 9}$ works. If you use these commands, it is a good idea to check the cursor location afterward.

Editing entries   The AppleWorks editing tools you learned in Part B work almost the same way with data base files. You can delete an entry by moving the cursor to the right and then using the $\boxed{\text{DELETE}}$ key. You can also move the cursor to the first character of the entry and use the Yank command $\boxed{\circ\ Y}$. This command deletes characters from the cursor to the end of the entry *not* the end of the line. Once an entry is deleted, you can type a new entry on the keyboard.

▪ Sorting Data Base Files

The real power of any data base program is in its commands for reorganizing data. AppleWorks allows you to sort all records into a new order. It also allows you to view certain selected records.

Sorting records   In AppleWorks, the Arrange command is $\boxed{\circ\ A}$. It changes the order of all records in a file. To use the command, you first move the cursor to the category containing the entries you want to sort. Then you give the command $\boxed{\circ\ A}$. Next, the computer asks what order to sort into: alphabetical, reverse alphabetical, numerical, or reverse numerical. After you choose, the computer moves whole records until they are in the order you asked for.

Getting answers   The ability to sort data base files is the key to getting certain kinds of information. An alphabetical sort on names makes it easy to locate a name you are looking for. A sort on numbers is the first step in finding the largest or smallest entries in a given category. In Session 8, you used sorting to answer questions such as these:

1. What is the state with the fifth smallest population?
2. What is the state with the fourth coldest winter?
3. What was the first state to join the Union after the original 13 colonies?

Need for sorting tools   Without a simple tool for sorting a data base, you would need to spend much time and effort to get answers to questions like these. Even with small data bases, such as States, the work would go slowly and might contain errors.

▪ Searching for Information

Not all questions about information in a data base file can be answered just by sorting it into a new order. In fact, with very large data bases, sorting is impractical because of the time required. Furthermore, sorting does not answer all questions. For example, if you want to find all the data for both North Dakota and South Dakota, alphabetizing the state names will not help. But searching for all records that contain Dakota will do the job.

The Find command In working with word processor files, you used the Find command `⌘ F` to find words, phrases, or any other text. This command works almost the same way with data base files. The main differences are these:

1. There is no `Case sensitive text` option when the command is used with data base files. In other words, the computer treats uppercase letters and lowercase letters in the same way.

2. The Find command causes the computer to show *all* data base records that contain the text you are searching for. The other records disappear from view temporarily.

The Find command is useful when you are searching for text that you know is located somewhere in a file. However, there are other kinds of searches that you can do.

Selecting records When you first put a data base file into the computer, all records are **selected**. This means that you can see all records in the file, either on the screen or by scrolling. Sometimes you want to select only certain records. For example, in the data base `States`, you might want to see records in which

1. Population is between two million and four million
2. Or, population is greater than one million and area is less than 20 thousand square miles
3. Or, either the summer temperature is less than 70 degrees or else the winter temperature is greater than 60

Selection rules Using only the tools described so far, you cannot easily find these records. Sorting is not enough nor is the Find command. Instead, you must define a new selection rule that tells the computer exactly which records you want to see. For example, the selection rule for example 3 above would look like this on the computer screen:

```
Selection: Jul is less than 70
   or         Jan is greater than 60
```

The Select Record command To create a new selection rule in AppleWorks, you must give the Select Record command `⌘ R`. After that, the computer prompts you for each **condition** that you want in the selection rule. There are two conditions shown in the selection rule above: The first is `Jul is less than 70`. The second is `Jan is greater than 60`. The meaning of the word "condition" is any phrase that can be either true or false. If you have studied programming, you have used conditions in the `IF` statement, which appears in BASIC, Logo, and most other languages.

The "or" connection When you have more than one condition in a selection rule, you must tell the computer how to combine them. In the example above, the word `or` connects the two conditions. This means that the computer should select a record if the first condition is true, *or* if the second condition is true, *or* if both conditions are true. If you are familiar with programming, the word "or" means the same thing in AppleWorks that it does in most programming languages.

The "and" connection Another connecting word is `and`. Here is a selection rule that uses `and`.

```
Selection: Population is greater than 1,000,000
and Area is less than 20,000
```

With this rule, a record is selected only if *both* conditions are true at the same time. Again, if you know a programming language, "and" means the same thing in AppleWorks.

Building selection rules AppleWorks makes the job of writing selection rules easy. Once you give the ⌘R command, the computer prompts you for each condition and each connecting word, one at a time. First, you choose the category name. Next, you choose the type of condition from a list of all possible conditions, written in simple English. Then, you complete the condition by entering a number or word. Finally, if there is more than one condition, the computer prompts for a connecting word and the next condition.

Seeing the results When your selection rule is complete, you tap ESC to see the selected records. You need not remember all the steps in building a new rule. Simply give the ⌘R command and follow the prompts. Then tap ESC when the rule is complete.

▪ Making Your Own Data Base

In the next hands-on session, you will enter information into a new data base file of your own. It will contain a list of people you know. For each person, you will enter a last name, a first name, a birthdate, and a phone number. After you create the data base, you will be able to sort it alphabetically by names or chronologically by birthdates. You will also be able to search for all people with birthdates in March, for example.

What you will need Before you begin working at the computer in

Session 10, make the following preparations. Write a list of 10 or more friends and family members. After each name on your list, write the person's birthdate and phone number. Remember to have your list with you when you begin working on the next session.

QUESTIONS

1. What is the main difference between a data base file and a word processor file?

2. What special term is used for the column headings you see when a data base file is shown on the REVIEW/ADD/CHANGE screen?

3. What special term is used for rows you see when a data base file is shown on the REVIEW/ADD/CHANGE screen?

4. What does the term "entry" mean?

5. What is the difference between the way the ⬅ and ➡ keys work in a data base file and a word processor file?

6. What key moves the cursor from entry to entry in a data base file?

7. Suppose the third category in a data base file is a person's last name. You want to sort the file so that last names are in alphabetical order. What are the first two steps you should take?

8. What is an example of a question you can answer by sorting the data base file States?

9. Sorting is one way to help find information in a data base file. What are two other ways? What commands must you use in each case?

10. What is the purpose of a selection rule?

11. What are the main parts of a selection rule called?

12. A selection rule contains two phrases: Age is greater than 21, Sex equals Female. Suppose the word and separates the two phrases. Describe the records that will be selected by this rule.

13. Suppose the word or separates the two phrases given in question 12. What records will be selected by this rule?

More Data Base Tools

SESSION GOALS:
- Explore the single-record layout of a data base file.
- Add and delete records in a data base file.
- Create a new data base file.
- Add a category to a data base file.

▪ Another View of a Data Base File

In Session 8, you learned how to change an entry in a data base file. You can also add whole records to or delete whole records from a file, and you can add whole categories or delete whole categories from a file. To do some of these things, you need a different way to look at the file.

Start the computer with AppleWorks as usual.

Put the data base file States **on the Desktop.**

You should be at the REVIEW/ADD/CHANGE screen with the state names in alphabetical order.

Move the cursor to Texas.

Then use the (TAB) **key to move the cursor over to** Austin.

You have made cursor moves like this before. Now, here is something new.

Give the Zoom command (ɕ̇ | Z).

This command "zooms" you in to the record on which you see the cursor. Here, the record contains all the data for Texas. This view of the file is called the **single-record layout**. Notice the labels before each entry in the record.

Give the Zoom command again.

You are back at the table form of the file with the Texas record now at the top. This view of the file is called the **multi-record layout**. Note the category names at the top of the table.

Give the (ɕ̇ | Z) **command.**

When you zoom in on a single record, each entry is labeled by the category names that appear in the multi-record layout.

Note where the cursor is. Tap the (TAB) **key.**

As in the multi-record layout, the (TAB) key moves the cursor to the next entry in the record. Similarly, (ɕ̇ | TAB) moves the cursor to the previous entry in the record.

Note the record number above the category names. Then tap the `TAB` **key to move the cursor to the last entry. Now tap** `TAB` **once more.**

As in the multi-record layout, if the cursor is at the last entry of a record, the `TAB` key moves it to the first entry in the next record. You can see that the record number has increased by one.

Tap the `↓` **key a few times.**

In the single-record layout, the `↑` and `↓` keys have the same effect as the `TAB` key. That is, they move the cursor from entry to entry, *not* from record to record.

Tap the `ú ↑` **key a few times. Try the** `ú ↓` **key.**

As you see, these commands move the cursor a record at a time when used with the single-record layout.

Give the `ú 9` **command. Give the** `ú 1` **command.**

These commands work exactly as in the multi-record layout. They move to the last record or the first record in the file.

1. What is the purpose of the `ú Z` command?
2. What does the `↓` key do in the multi-record layout? What does it do in the single-record layout?

▪ Adding Records

In Session 8, you learned how to change individual entries in a record. Sometimes, you need to add whole new records to the data base file and delete whole old records when they are no longer needed. The data base program in AppleWorks has tools for adding and deleting records.

As it stands, the data base file States has records for each of the states and the District of Columbia. Suppose you want to add a record for Puerto Rico and one for the Virgin Islands. Here are the steps:

Use `ú 9` **to move the cursor to the last record in the file.**

You should now be in the single-record layout. Note the **record indicator** above the row of equal signs. It should say Record 51 of 51. This record is the last one in the file.

Tap the `TAB` **key until the cursor is at the last entry in the record. Tap** `TAB` **once more.**

In the middle of the screen, you should see the following message:

```
You are now past the last record
of your file and can now start
typing new records at the end.
```

The prompt at the bottom of the screen asks if you really want to add records. If you moved the cursor beyond the last record by accident, you would tap Ⓝ to correct the mistake. However, you do want to add records.

Tap Ⓨ to confirm that you do want to add records.

The computer tells you that you are now at record 52 of 52. It shows all the category names, but the entries are all blank. The computer is waiting for you to enter the data for record 52.

Type Puerto Rico. **Use the (DELETE) key to fix any errors. Then tap (RETURN).**

You have just entered the State Name for this record. The cursor is at the second category name.

Type 3,196,520 **and tap (RETURN).**

Enter 3,435 **for the area.**

Enter San Juan **for the capital.**

Enter 76 **for the January temperature and** 81 **for July.**

You have now entered all of the data available for Puerto Rico. Because it has not been admitted to the Union, we will leave the last entry blank.

Tap (RETURN) for a blank entry.

That finishes record 52, and the computer automatically moves on to record 53, which is also blank.

Enter the following data for record 53:

```
Name: Virgin Islands
Population: 95,000
Area: 133
Capital: Charlotte Amalie
Jan: 76
Jul: 81
Admitted:
```

That finishes record 53. You should now be looking at record 54 of 54. The computer is waiting for more data. You have finished adding records, so it is time to go back to the REVIEW/ADD/CHANGE screen.

Tap (ESC).

Now, let us look at the file in the multi-record layout.

Give the (ɔ|Z) command.

The computer shows you the last of the old records plus the two new ones you just added.

Tap the ⬇ key until you hear a beep.

In the multi-record layout, you cannot move the cursor beyond the last record. Whenever you want to add records, you must use the single-record layout.

Right now, the new records you have added are at the end of the file. However, you can use the Arrange command to put the new records where you want them. For example, you can sort the file alphabetically by name.

Make sure the cursor is in the Name column. Give the Arrange command ⌘A. Sort the file From A to Z.

Move the cursor to the end of the file.

Now Puerto Rico and Virgin Islands are in their proper alphabetical order.

Use the TAB key to put the cursor in the Jul temperature column.

Sort the file so that the highest July temperatures come first.

If everything went well, you see the record for Arizona at the top of the screen. Two-thirds of the way down, you should see the records for Puerto Rico and the Virgin Islands.

3. Suppose you are looking at a data base file in the multi-record layout. What are the first two steps needed to add a record at the end of the file?

4. What key must you press after you type each entry in a record?

5. How do you tell the computer there are no more records to be added?

▪ Deleting Records

It is easy enough to add records to a data base file. Deleting records is even simpler. Let us suppose you want the file to contain only records for the 50 states. You must delete three records: the two you just added and the one for the District of Columbia.

Be sure you are using the multi-record layout to display the file.

Move the cursor anywhere within the record for Puerto Rico.

Give the Delete command ⌘D.

That causes the computer to highlight the entire record containing the cursor. You are now at the Delete Records screen.

Tap the (ESC) key.

The highlighting is gone, and you are back at the REVIEW/ADD/
CHANGE screen. As usual, the (ESC) key undoes the command.

**With the cursor in the Puerto Rico record, give the Delete command
again.**

Read the prompt at the bottom of the screen.

Tap (↓) to highlight the next record.

You have now selected the records for Puerto Rico and the Virgin
Islands. They are ready to be deleted.

Tap (RETURN).

That is all there is to it. The two records are no longer part of file
States.

**Use the same method to delete the record for the District of
Columbia.**

**Put the cursor in the last record of the file. Use (⌀|Z) to zoom in on
that record.**

You should be looking at record 50 of 50, the last record in the file.

6. Suppose you are looking at a file in the multi-record layout. What
   are the first two steps in deleting a record?
7. How does the computer show which records are going to be deleted?

• Creating a New Data Base File

You now know all the important tools for working with an existing data
base file. You know how to search for information, how to arrange the
file in different order, how to change entries in a record, how to add new
records, and how to delete records. However, there is one very important tool that is missing. You do not yet know how to create a new data
base file from scratch. You will learn how to do that next.

**Go to the Main Menu. Remove the file States from the Desktop.
When prompted, throw out the changes you made to the file.**

At the end of Session 9, you were told to put together a list of your
friends' names, their phone numbers, and their birthdates. Now you
will use some of this information to create a data base called "People."

Give the Add files command from the Main Menu.

This time, you will not be getting a file from your disk. Instead, you will
make a new data base file from scratch.

Give the Data Base **and** From scratch **commands.**

When prompted, type the name People **and tap** (RETURN).

You should now see the following screen:

```
File: People          CHANGE NAME/CATEGORY    Escape: Review/Add/Change


Category names
─────────────────────────────────────────────────────────────
Category 1

                                    Options:

                                    Change category name
                                    Up arrow    Go to filename
                                    Down arrow  Go to next category
                                    A-I         Insert new category




─────────────────────────────────────────────────────────────
Type entry or use ⌂ commands                        55K Avail.
```

Creating a new data base file always begins at this screen. The computer is waiting for you to type the category names you want. For now, you will make a data base file with only three category names: Last Name, First Name, and Birthdate.

Give the Yank command (⌂ Y) **to delete the name** Category 1.

Type Last Name **and tap** (RETURN).

The cursor is on the next line. The computer is waiting for you to type the next category name.

Type First Name **and tap** (RETURN).

Type Birthdate. **Be sure to spell this correctly. Then tap** (RETURN).

You have now entered the three category names to be used in your new data base file. If you made any typing errors, you can use the (↑) key to move the cursor to the line containing the error. Then you can use any of the editing tools to fix the error.

When you have the category names you wish, you must tell the computer that there are no more names and you are ready to begin entering data.

Tap (ESC).

You are now at the REVIEW/ADD/CHANGE screen. In the middle of the screen you should see the following message:

```
This file does not yet contain
any information. Therefore, you
will automatically go into the
Insert New Records feature.
```

Follow the directions at the bottom of the screen.

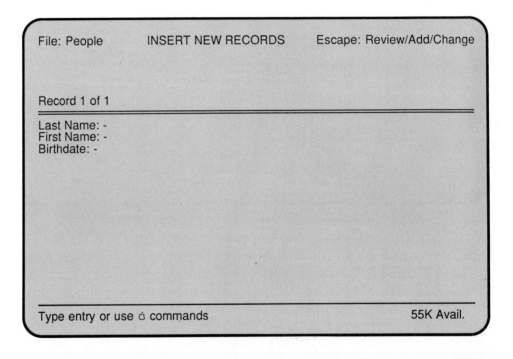

```
File: People          INSERT NEW RECORDS          Escape: Review/Add/Change



Record 1 of 1
─────────────────────────────────────────────────────────────────────────
Last Name: -
First Name: -
Birthdate: -








─────────────────────────────────────────────────────────────────────────
Type entry or use ⨁ commands                                     55K Avail.
```

You have seen this kind of screen before. It is the single-record layout of the file People. However, there are no entries in the file yet. The computer is waiting for you to type entries for the first person on your list. At the end of Session 9, you were asked to make a list of people and their birthdates.

Get out your list of people and birthdates.

Type the last name of the first person on your list. Fix errors with the (DELETE) key. Then tap (RETURN).

Type the person's first name and tap (RETURN).

Type the person's birthdate in the form Dec 16 **and tap** (RETURN).

Now you have entered all the data for record 1. The computer is waiting for you to enter the data for the second person on your list.

Repeat the previous three steps for the second person.

Keep entering data until you have five complete records. Then tap (ESC).

Now you are back at the REVIEW/ADD/CHANGE screen, but the computer is still using the single-record layout.

Use the Zoom command (ɔ|Z) **to see the whole file.**

You should now see the five records of file People. The records are in the order you entered them. However, this is a data base file and you can rearrange it using the (ɔ|A) command.

Place the cursor in the First Name **column. Give the Arrange command, and sort alphabetically.**

Place the cursor in the Birthdate **column. Give the Arrange command, and sort chronologically.**

As with the other data base files you have used, the Arrange command lets you change the order of records. You have done alphabetical and numerical sorts before. The **chronological** sort is new. Whenever a category name contains the word "date," the computer interprets your entries in that category as dates. Chronological order means from earliest date to latest date.

8. Suppose you have told the computer you want to create a new data base file from scratch. You have also entered a name for the file. What information must you enter next?

9. How do you tell the computer you want to sort a category in chronological order (by date)?

▪ Adding a New Category

When you are creating a new data base file, you sometimes forget a category that you later want to add to the file. For example, you might want your People file to contain phone numbers as well as the other types of information already entered. Here is how to add a whole new category to a data base file.

Give the Name command (ɔ|N).

You are now back at the Change Name/Category screen. This screen is the one you used to enter the original category names. This screen also allows you to do other things. Right now, the computer is waiting for you to change the file name if you want to. But you do not want to do this now. The message in the middle of the screen tells you what to do.

Tap (RETURN).

The message on the screen shows you the other things you can do. You can change a category name, insert a whole new category, or delete an old category. You want to insert a new category. You will put it just before the Birthdate category.

Use the (↓) key to put the cursor on Birthdate.

Give the Insert command (ᵹ I).

The list of category names opened up and the computer is now waiting for you to type the new category name.

Use the Yank command (ᵹ Y) to delete the hyphen in the blank line.

Type Phone and tap (RETURN).

Tap (ESC).

Now you have the new Phone category in the file, but you are still missing the data. Now it is time to enter the phone numbers from the list you made before beginning this session.

Move the cursor to the first record, third column. Type the phone number that belongs there in the form 555-1212. Then tap (RETURN).

Repeat this process until all the phone numbers have been entered.

Now each record in the file contains a new entry, the phone number. This completes your data base. If you have time later, you may want to add more records or more categories to it.

Go back to the Main Menu and save file People on your Computer Applications DATA Disk.

This completes your work with the data base program. If you have time, do some of the On Your Own activities. Then quit the computer as usual.

10. What command must you use when you want to add a whole new category to a data base?

11. After you type the command in question 10, what four things can you do to a data base file?

- Clear the Desktop if necessary. Move a copy of the file States from your Computer Applications DATA Disk to the Desktop. Change to the single-record layout. Practice using all the cursor-move commands you know. Return to the multi-record layout. Give the ⌥ N command. Change the file name to Union. Delete the category Capital. When you are finished, remove the file from the Desktop and throw out your changes.

- Clear the Desktop if necessary. Move the file People from the disk to the Desktop. Add records for the rest of the people on the list you made before beginning this session. Save the file on your disk.

- If necessary, put the file People on the Desktop. Add a new Age category to the file. Enter data for the ages you know, and leave the rest blank.

Using Data Bases

SESSION GOALS:
- Compare the single-record and multi-record layouts available with AppleWorks data base files.
- Review the steps for adding and deleting records in a data base file.
- Learn commands for moving and copying blocks of records.
- Review the steps for creating a new data base and adding new categories to an existing data base.
- Learn to remove a category, change the layout, and print reports.
- Learn about the role of data bases in society.

▪ The Two Layouts

There is only one way to view a word processor file on the REVIEW/ADD/CHANGE screen. The text appears, one line after the other, from the beginning to the end of the file. However, there are two quite different ways to view a data base file on the REVIEW/ADD/CHANGE screen.

Multi-record layout In one view, a data base file appears as a table with rows and columns. Each row contains the entries for a single record in the file. Each column contains all the entries that belong to one category. This view is called the *multi-record layout.*

Single-record layout In the other view, all the entries for a single record appear on the screen. Each row in the display shows one category name and the entry for that category. This view is called the *single-record layout.* In many data base programs, the single-record layout is the only one available.

The Zoom command With AppleWorks, you can view your data either way. It is up to you to decide which view you want. You use the Zoom command ⌐ⓒ│Z⌐ to switch from either view to the other. When you zoom from a multi-record layout to a single-record layout, you see the record that the cursor was on when you gave the Zoom command. When you zoom back, the record that appears in the single-record layout will be the top line in the multi-record view. The other records are still there, and you can scroll to see them.

Advantages and disadvantages The best feature of the multi-record layout is that it lets you see entries for as many as 15 records at the same time. At a glance, you can compare entries in different records. However, your data base file may contain too many categories to fit on a single line on the screen. When this happens in multi-record layout, only the first few categories are visible. There is no easy way in

AppleWorks to bring the other columns of the table into view. The single-record layout shows entries for only one record at a time, but all categories are visible. Each layout serves a purpose.

■ Adding Whole Records

Changing an entry in a data base record is easy. In the multi-record layout, you move the cursor to the entry, delete it, type the new entry, and tap (RETURN). Creating a whole new record is a bit more complicated.

Putting records at the end One way to add records is to go past the end of the file and type the new entries. The computer will not allow you to move the cursor past the last record in the multi-record layout. Therefore, you must switch to the single-record layout. When you move the cursor past the last record, the computer prompts you to type each entry for a new record. You may add several new records this way.

Putting records in the middle AppleWorks also allows you to insert a new record in the middle of a file. You did not do this at the computer, but the steps are simple. First, you choose the record ahead of which you want the new record to be inserted. Then, using either layout, you move the cursor to that record. Finally, you give the Insert command (ᵓ I) and type the new entries when prompted.

Which method is best? No matter which method you use for adding records, the new records become a part of the data base file. If you sort the file, the new records will be sorted into new locations along with the old records. Usually, it makes no difference whether you add records to the end or insert them in the middle. The one exception occurs when you are building a data base file that will never be sorted into a new order. In that case, you should use the Insert command to put a record where you want it.

■ Block Editing

In your work with word processor files, you used commands for deleting, moving, and copying whole blocks of text. These same AppleWorks commands work with data base files. The only difference is that in a data base file, the blocks are made up of whole records.

Deleting a block The Delete command (ᵓ D) lets you delete one or more records from a data base file. To use the command in the multi-record layout, you place the cursor at either the first or the last record in the block you want to delete. Then you give the command and move the cursor to the other end of the block. The computer highlights all records you have selected. Finally, you tap (RETURN), and the records are erased from the file.

Moving a block Although you did not use it, the Move command

$\boxed{\acute{\texttt{o}}\,|\,\text{M}}$ also works with data base files. You select records exactly as with the Delete command. Then you put the cursor where you want the records to be moved. When you tap $\boxed{\text{RETURN}}$, the move is made. As with the Insert command, the Move command is useful only with files that will not be sorted into a new order. If you intend to sort a file, it does not matter what order the records are in before sorting.

Copying a block   You did not use the Copy command $\boxed{\acute{\texttt{o}}\,|\,\text{C}}$ either. It works the same way as the Move command, except that a duplicate copy of the selected records is moved to the new location. This command can be useful when you want to create a new record that is similar to an existing one. You simply make a copy and then edit the copy.

▪ Creating a New Data Base

When you use a word processor program, most of your time goes into entering text into the computer. With a data base program, most time is spent getting information out of an existing data base file. Nevertheless, once in a while you will want to create an entire new data base of your own. All data base programs have tools for this job.

Getting started   The first steps for creating a new data base file from scratch are the same as for creating a new word processor or spreadsheet file. In all cases, you go to the Main Menu and use the Add files command. Instead of asking for a disk file, you say that you want to make a new file. At this point, you say what kind of file it will be. Then you say that you want to make the file from scratch, and you enter a name for the file.

Entering categories   If you have chosen to make a data base file, the computer goes to the Change Name/Category screen and prompts for the names you want for your categories. You simply type each one and tap $\boxed{\text{RETURN}}$. This screen also allows you to edit category names, insert new categories, and delete old ones. You can even change the file name. After the category names are entered, you tap $\boxed{\text{ESC}}$.

Entering records   The computer then moves automatically to the Insert New Records screen. (The Insert command $\boxed{\acute{\texttt{o}}\,|\,\text{I}}$ also takes you to this screen.) The computer prompts you to enter all data for the first record. You type each entry and tap $\boxed{\text{RETURN}}$. When you make the last entry, the computer prompts for data for the second record. You continue in this way until all records are finished. Then you tap $\boxed{\text{ESC}}$ and go to the REVIEW/ADD/CHANGE screen, where you can see the new file in the multi-record layout.

▪ Adding and Deleting Categories

When creating a data base, you often think of whole new categories of information that you would like to have in the file. After using the file for a time, you may find that some categories are not used. Most data base programs have tools for adding new categories to an existing data base and removing unwanted categories.

Adding a category The ⌘N command takes you to the Change Name/Category screen, which shows all the categories. To insert a new one, you first place the cursor where the new category is to go and then give the ⌘I command. At the prompt, you delete the hyphen that appears there and type the new category name. Finally, you tap ESC.

Adding the data The computer now returns you to the REVIEW/ADD/CHANGE screen, where the new category shows up with blank entries. The next step is to enter data for that category in each record. In effect, you change the blanks into the new entries. You do this by moving the cursor to each blank, typing the entry, and tapping RETURN.

Deleting a category Erasing an existing category is much easier than adding a new one. The first step is to use the ⌘N command to go to the Change Name/Category screen. Next, you move the cursor to the name of the category to be deleted. Then you give the Delete command ⌘D. The computer warns that the entries in that category will be erased permanently from the file. You finish by saying that you really want the category to be deleted.

▪ Other Data Base Tools

This has been a brief introduction to the use of the AppleWorks data base program. You have used all the main commands for creating a new data base, changing entries, and finding information. The AppleWorks data base program has other data base tools that you may want to use for special tasks. See the AppleWorks reference manual for details about these tools.

▪ Other Data Bases

Although you have been using one data base program, you have learned the important ideas for working with any other data base program. The command names will probably be different. The order in which you do things will also be different. But the basic ideas will be the same.

Records and categories All data base files can be thought of as a table with rows and columns. The rows are usually called *records* and the columns are usually called *categories*. Sometimes the terms are different. A data base program that has only the single-record layout often refers to a record as a "form" and to the category names as "item names." Other data base programs use the terms "attributes" or "fields" for categories. However, these different terms all refer to the same ideas: rows and columns of data.

Sorting by categories Most data base programs have commands that allow you to *sort* a file according to the entries in a given category. These commands will look different from one another, and they will be used differently. But they all serve the same purpose: to sort records into a new order that helps you find answers to questions.

Searching Most data base programs have other commands that allow you to give the computer a rule for *selecting* records in a file. Again, the way you do these things will vary, but the purpose will be the same: to find useful information.

Printing reports All data base programs have commands for printing reports based on the data in a file. After you select the records you want and the categories of data you want to see, you can tell the computer to print the information neatly in whatever form you ask.

Adding and changing data All data base programs have a way to add new records to a data base file, add new categories, remove records and categories, and change entries in a record. The people responsible for keeping the data base up to date use these tools often. Other people who merely use the data do not need to make changes. Many data base programs have ways to prevent some users from making any changes at all to the data base.

▪ Public Use of Data Bases

You have been using data base files that were contained in your own computer. You were the only user of the files. Many data bases are kept in a single location and are used by hundreds or thousands of people.

An example If you want to go to a concert, you often can go to many different places to buy a ticket. Each ticket seller has a **terminal** connected to a computer. Inside the computer, there is a data base file containing information about ticket prices and availability. When you buy a ticket, the data base is changed to show that the ticket is no longer available.

Security and privacy When important information is kept in a data base file, it is natural to worry about losing the information. You may not want certain information to fall into other people's hands. These concerns are especially important in a central data base that many people use. Often, such systems give each user a special secret **password**. The password must be entered into the computer before the user can gain access to the data base. Only certain users may see certain information.

Data bases in the future Many experts believe that the main use of personal computers in the future will be to communicate with remote data bases. They believe that such data bases will be new sources of information and will give new services. People at home may be able to search for jobs, make purchases, check to see what is at the movies, make airline reservations, and do many other things by using a home computer as a terminal for a data base miles away. If so, people will be doing many of the things you have learned here.

QUESTIONS

1. What are the advantages and disadvantages of the multi-record layout?

2. What are the advantages and disadvantages of the single-record layout?

3. What AppleWorks command allows you to add new records in the middle of a data base file?

4. Usually it does not matter where you add new records to a data base file. Why?

5. Suppose a new planet is discovered. You want to put the information into your Planets file. What kind of change must you make to the file?

6. Suppose a new moon is discovered for the planet Jupiter. The planet is already in your data base file. What kind of change must you make to put the new information in your file?

7. You can use the Delete command ⌐á|D⌐ with both word processor files and data base files when they are on the REVIEW/ADD/CHANGE screen. For each type of file, what things are deleted by the command?

8. When creating a new data base file, the first information you enter is a name for the file. What type of information must you enter after that?

9. Suppose you want to add information to your Planets file. For each planet, you want to add the time needed for a rocket to travel there from Earth. What type of change must you make to the file? What AppleWorks command would you use to start the change?

10. What are two ways that most data base programs let you get information from a file?

11. How does the use of passwords make a data base more secure?

12. What are three possible data bases that people might communicate with from their homes by means of personal computers?

▪ Menu Commands

and   A connecting word used in building a selection rule. Both conditions on either side of the word must be true for a record to be selected.

or   A connecting word used in building a selection rule. Either condition or both conditions must be true for a record to be selected.

through   A connecting word used in building a selection rule. The selection rule specifies a range of values for which records will be selected.

▪ Keyboard Commands

TAB   Move the cursor to the next entry in a data base file.

⌘ A , Arrange   Arrange or sort a data base file according to the entries in one category.

⌘ C , Copy   Make one or more copies of a record in a data base file. The copies are inserted immediately after the original record.

⌘ D , Delete   Delete records or categories in a data base file.

⌘ F , Find   Find and display all records containing the text you type.

⌘ I , Insert   Insert records or categories in a data base file.

⌘ L , Layout   Change the arrangement of categories in a record.

⌘ M , Move   Move one or more records to a new location in a data base file.

⌘ N , Name   Change the name of a file or a category.

⌘ R , Record selection   Change record selection rules. Only selected records appear on the REVIEW/ADD/CHANGE screen.

⌘ TAB   Move the cursor to the previous entry in a data base file.

⌘ Y , Yank   Erase characters from the cursor to the end of an entry.

⌘ Z , Zoom   Change from multi-record layout to single-record layout or vice versa.

▪ New Ideas

category   A word or phrase that describes one kind of information in a data base file. In the multi-record layout, each column contains one category of information. A category is sometimes called a "field."

entry   A single item of data in a data base file. Each entry belongs to one category and one record.

multi-record layout   A table with rows and columns. Each row contains the information for one record. Each column contains the information in one category or field.

password   A security measure to keep unauthorized people from using data base files or other information in computer systems.

record   All the information about a single object in a data base file. A data base file consists of many records.

selection rule   A rule used by the computer to decide whether to pick a record out of a data base file.

single-record layout   A screen display that shows all the information in one record in a data base file. In many data base programs, this is the only display available.

sort alphabetically   Arrange records so that entries in one category are in alphabetical order.

sort chronologically   Arrange records so that entries in one category are in date order. This order is available only if the category name contains the word "date."

sort numerically   Arrange records so that entries in one category are in numerical order.

The Spreadsheet Program

In Part B, you used a word processor program to help you with writing tasks. In Part C, you learned how a data base program helps you organize information, sort it, and find facts. Part D deals with another important computer application—a spreadsheet program. It helps you create tables of numbers and do calculations with the numbers in the table.

Similarities to data bases When you first see a spreadsheet file on the computer screen, you will probably think it is just another data base file. In many ways, they are alike. For example, the information is organized the same way in both kinds of files: You can think of either kind of file as a table made up of entries that are arranged in rows and columns. Most of the AppleWorks tools for dealing with data base files work the same way with spreadsheet files.

Differences from data bases Spreadsheet files are mainly collections of numbers. A spreadsheet program gives you special tools for working with the numbers in a table. These tools make it easy for you to add a column of numbers, calculate an average, or multiply two numbers. You cannot do these things with most data base programs, although a few programs mix data base tools with spreadsheet tools.

Spreadsheet tools In Part D, you will learn to use the special tools in AppleWorks for doing calculations with numbers that appear in tables. You will see how the spreadsheet program can be used to simplify many different jobs. You will work with sports statistics, recipes, multiplication tables, and grocery lists. This will give you an idea of the many different applications of the spreadsheet program.

Exploring Spreadsheets

▪ Making a New Spreadsheet File

In Parts B and C, you explored a word processor program and a data base program. In this session, you will begin exploring a **spreadsheet program**. First, you must create an empty spreadsheet file on the Desktop.

Start the computer with your AppleWorks disks as usual. At the Main Menu, give the `Add files` **command.**

At the Add Files menu, select `Spreadsheet` **and tap** `RETURN`**. Make the new file from scratch.**

When prompted, type the file name `Calculate` **and tap** `RETURN`**.**

The figure on page 103 shows what your screen should look like. An empty spreadsheet file always appears this way.

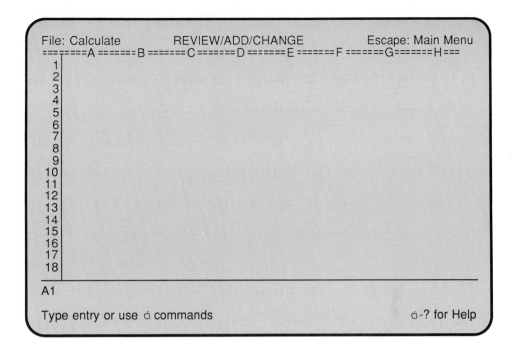

```
File: Calculate          REVIEW/ADD/CHANGE          Escape: Main Menu
=======A =======B =======C =======D =======E =======F =======G=======H===
 1
 2
 3
 4
 5
 6
 7
 8
 9
10
11
12
13
14
15
16
17
18
_____
A1

Type entry or use ⌂ commands                         ⌂-? for Help
```

As with the other two application programs you have used, the computer shows the contents of the file on the REVIEW/ADD/CHANGE screen. Each type of file looks slightly different on this screen.

Look at the top and left borders of the screen.

When the computer displays a spreadsheet file, you will always see a row of letters across the top and a column of numbers down the left side. Any information in the file will show up in the area below the letters and to the right of the numbers. As you see, there is nothing there now because the file is empty.

1. What screen must you be on to enter information into an empty spreadsheet file?
2. What information on the screen tells you that you are looking at a spreadsheet file?

▪ Moving the Cell Cursor

The large highlighted rectangle at the upper left corner of the screen is called the **cell cursor**. In Parts B and C, you learned commands for moving the regular cursor through a word processor or data base file. These same commands move the cell cursor through a spreadsheet file.

Note the letter and number at the bottom left corner of the screen.

Tap the ⟶ key and look again at the letter and number.

Tap the ↓ key and look once more at the letter and number.

The letter and number should now read B2. The letter B stands for the second column on the spreadsheet. The number 2 stands for the second row. The combination B2 is a **cell name**. The place on the screen that shows the cell name is called the **cell indicator**.

Move the cursor to cell E14. Check the cell indicator to make sure it is there.

Move the cursor to cell C4.

You can use the four arrow keys to move the cell cursor wherever you like on the screen.

Give the command ⌘ ⟶. Then use ⌘ ⟵.

As you probably guessed, these commands cause large horizontal jumps.

Give the command ⌘ ↑. Then try ⌘ ↓. Use ⌘ ↓ a second time.

When the cell cursor is on the bottom row of the screen, ⌘ ↓ brings the next 18 rows into view on the screen. The file Calculate has no information in those cells either.

Give the command ⌘ 1.

As usual, this command brings the beginning of the file into view. What do you think the command ⌘ 9 does?

Try ⌘ 9.

That was probably a surprise. This command moves the cell cursor to the last row containing any information. Since your file has no information, the cell cursor stays on the top row. But you saw earlier that there are many empty rows below that one.

Hold the ↓ key down for a while.

Hold both ⌘ and ↓ down until you hear a beep.

The beep means that there are no more rows available. The bottom row of an AppleWorks spreadsheet is number 999.

Use ⌘ 1 to return to the top of the file. Move to cell H1.

While watching the row of letters at the top of the screen, tap ⟶ slowly a few times.

This is new. Each tap of the ⟶ key caused the row of letters to move to the left. As columns A and B of the spreadsheet disappear, new columns I and J show up at the right. This is called **horizontal scrolling**. With word processor and data base files, you can scroll vertically but not horizontally. With a spreadsheet file, you can scroll in either direction.

Scroll horizontally to cell Z1. Tap ⟶ a few more times.

The new column labels have two letters. The first is A and the second starts through the alphabet again.

While watching the column labels, use the ⟨ᴄ́|→⟩ command to scroll as far to the right as possible.

The beep announces that there are no more columns. The last column is DW. This is the 127th column.

Use ⟨ᴄ́|←⟩ to go back to cell A1.

3. Suppose the cursor is at cell D7. At which row and column is the cell located?

4. If the cell cursor is in a column at the right edge of the screen, what does the command ⟨ᴄ́|→⟩ do?

▪ Looking at Cells

As you see, moving the cell cursor though a spreadsheet file is similar to moving the regular cursor through a word processor or a data base file. Now you will see how to put information inside cells.

Move the cursor to cell B3.

The cell indicator should show that the cursor is indeed at B3. The prompt at the bottom of the screen says that you can enter information by typing it. You will be entering the word "hello."

With your eye on the cell indicator, tap the ⟨H⟩ key. (If you make a mistake, tap ⟨ESC⟩ and start over.)

The lower left corner of your screen should look like this:

```
- - - - - - - - - - - - -
B3
Label: h
Complete the label
```

When you tap the ⟨H⟩ key, the computer decides that you want to enter a type of information called a **label**. You now see the letter you typed in two places. It follows the word Label at the bottom of the screen. It also appears inside the cell cursor at location B3.

The message at the bottom of the screen tells you to type the rest of the characters in the label. When you tap ⟨RETURN⟩, the label is complete.

Watch the screen carefully while you type the letters `ello`**. If you make a mistake, use the** `DELETE` **key to erase the incorrect letters.**

When the label is correct, tap `RETURN`**.**

You have now entered information into the spreadsheet. You can see the information in two places: in cell `B3` and in the cell indicator at the bottom of the screen.

Move the cursor down a few cells.

As you can see, the label `hello` remains visible in cell `B3`. The cell indicator shows that the new cell has nothing in it.

Move the cursor to cell `C5`**.**

In addition to labels, you can also enter numbers in spreadsheet cells. You will enter the number `23` next.

Tap the `2` **key. (If you make a mistake, tap** `ESC` **and start over.)**

The lower left corner of your screen should look like this:

```
- - - - - - - - - - - - -
C5
Value: 2
Complete the value
```

When you tapped the `2` key, the computer decided that you wanted to enter a type of information called a **value**. You now see the number you typed in only one place. It follows the word `Value` at the bottom of the screen.

The message at the bottom of the screen tells you to type the rest of the digits in the number. When you tap `RETURN`, the number is complete.

Tap the `3` **key and then tap** `RETURN`**.**

As soon as you tap `RETURN`, the number you entered appears in the cell. The number also appears in the cell indicator at the bottom of the screen.

Move the cursor down a few cells.

As before, the information you entered stays in view on the spreadsheet cell when the cursor is moved.

Move the cursor back to cell `B3`**. Read the cell indicator.**

Move the cursor to cell `C5`**. Read the cell indicator.**

The cell indicator tells you that cell `B3` contains the *label* `hello` and cell `C5` contains the *value* `23`.

To review, *labels* and *values* are the two kinds of information you can enter into spreadsheet cells. Labels are sets of letters or other characters. Values are either numbers that you enter or numbers that are calculated by the computer.

If the first character you type is a letter, the computer assumes you want to enter a label. If it is a number, the computer assumes you are entering a value.

5. What two kinds of information can you enter into a spreadsheet cell?
6. How does the computer know what kind of information you are entering into a spreadsheet cell?
7. Suppose you start entering one kind of information into a cell and decide that it is the wrong type. What should you do?

▪ Calculating Cell Values

So far, a spreadsheet file looks very much like a data base file. Both have information arranged in rows and columns. The information can be words or numbers. Next you will see an important difference.

Move the cursor to cell D7. **Type the characters** 32+21 **and tap** RETURN.

The cell indicator tells you that cell D7 contains exactly what you typed. But on the spreadsheet, cell D7 contains the number 53. The number 53 is indeed the sum of 32 and 21.

Here is what is going on. The cell indicator always shows you what information is stored in the spreadsheet file itself. You entered the characters 32+21, and they are stored in cell D7 in the file. The computer looks in **file cell** D7 to decide what to display in **screen cell** D7. Since file cell D7 contains a **formula**, the computer calculates 32+21 and displays the sum 53 in screen cell D7.

Go to cell C9 **and enter the formula** 82*53.

You should see your formula in file cell C9 and the number 4346 in screen cell C9. The asterisk (*) stands for multiplication. The formula says to multiply 82 by 53.

Go to cell E5 **and enter the formula** 144/9.

Again, you should see the formula in the file cell and the result in the screen cell. The slash (/) stands for "divided by."

In cell B12, **tell the computer to subtract** 321 **from** 789.

In cell F9, **enter a formula for adding the numbers** 15, 31, **and** 45.

As you see, there is a big difference between a data base file and a spreadsheet file. With a data base file, what you see on the screen is what you entered into the file. However, formulas in a spreadsheet file let you tell the computer how to calculate the numbers that appear on the screen. You can use formulas that add, subtract, multiply, and divide numbers—just as if there were a pocket calculator in each cell.

So far, the screen cells have always shown the results of the formulas stored in the file cells. To see the formula in a cell, you had to move the cursor to that cell and then read the cell indicator. AppleWorks gives you a way to see all the formulas at once.

Give the Zoom command (Ᏻ|Z).

Now the formulas appear in the screen cells exactly as they are stored in the file cells.

Give the Zoom command again.

The command (Ᏻ|Z) switches back and forth between these two ways of looking at a spreadsheet file.

8. What information does the cell indicator show?

9. When is the information in a screen cell and a file cell the same? When is it different?

10. What command allows you to see all the formulas in a spreadsheet file?

▪ Editing Cells

As with all computer applications, you will spend much of your time editing information already in files. Editing a spreadsheet file usually means deleting information in cells and entering new information there.

Go to cell C9. **Type** bye, **but do not tap** (RETURN) **yet.**

The bottom left part of your screen should look like this:

```
- - - - - - - - - - - -
C9: (Value) 82*53
Label: bye
Complete the label
```

The first line below the dashed line shows what is now contained in file cell C9: the formula 82*53. The second line shows the three characters you just typed: the label bye. The third line prompts you to finish.

Tap (RETURN).

Now the file cell contains the label bye. The formula 82*53 stored there before is now deleted. (If you change your mind before tapping (RETURN), you can use (ESC) to leave the cell unchanged.)

Change cell B3 **to contain** 2001.

Sometimes you simply want to blank out the information in a file cell without inserting anything new. Here is how to do it:

Put the cursor at cell B12. **Give the Blank command** (ᴄ͞|B).

The prompt shows that you can blank out a single entry, a whole row of entries, a whole column of entries, or a rectangular block of entries.

Tap (RETURN) **to blank out the single entry.**

Cell B12 in the file is now blank. Here is how to delete entries in a block:

Put the cursor on cell C5. **Give the Blank command. Select** Block **and tap** (RETURN).

The screen prompt asks you to highlight the block of entries to be blanked out. You will select a three-by-three block.

Tap (→) **twice. Tap** (↓) **twice.**

You have selected a rectangle of nine cells, three of which contain information.

Tap (RETURN) **to blank out the block.**

Blank out the other entries in the file any way you like.

11. Suppose you want to change the entry in cell H16. What steps must you follow?
12. Suppose you want to blank out the entry in cell F3. What steps must you follow?

▪ A New Spreadsheet File

You have learned most of the main features of a spreadsheet file. However, you have not seen these features applied in a practical example. There are several simple ones on your Computer Applications DATA Disk.

Go to the Main Menu. Give the Remove files **command. Throw out the file** Calculate.

Give the Add files **and** current disk **commands. When prompted, swap disks.**

Scroll to the end of the directory.

All the spreadsheet files are located at the end of the directory.

Choose Multiply **and tap** (RETURN).

```
=======A ======= B ======= C ======= D ======= E ======= F ======= G ======= H ===
 1
 2
 3                               Multiplication Table
 4
 5                    5        6        7        8        9
 6          ============================================================
 7      5           25       30       35       40       45
 8      6           30       36       42       48       54
 9      7           35       42       49       56       63
10      8           40       48       56       64       72
11      9           45       54       63       72       81
12
13
14
15
16
17
18
```

A1

Type entry or use ó commands   ó-? for Help

This spreadsheet file contains a part of the standard multiplication table. Each entry in the table is the product of the number at the left of the table and the number at the top. Most things in this table will be familiar to you. But there is one important difference. Let us begin with the familiar things.

Find out what kind of information is stored in cells D3 through F3.

Find out what kind of information is stored in cells A7 through A11.

Check cell B11.

Like the earlier file with which you were working, this spreadsheet file contains labels and values.

Check cell C7.

This file cell contains the formula 5*5. The computer uses this formula to calculate the number 25 in the screen cell C7.

Look at cells C8, D7, and D8.

There is nothing unexpected here. Now let us look at something new.

See what is stored in file cell C11.

The cell indicator says that the formula +A11*C5 is stored in file cell

C11. Somehow, the computer uses this information to calculate the number 45, which you see in screen cell C11. The characters A11 and C5 in the formula look like cell names. Let us see what is in those cells.

Move the cursor to cell A11 and note the number there. Move the cursor to cell C5 and note that number.

Now you can see where 45 came from. The computer multiplied the 9 in cell A11 by the 5 in cell C5.

Move over to cell D11 and look at the formula stored in the file.

This time, the formula says to multiply the number in A11 times the number in D5. The result is 9 times 6, or 54, which is the number you see in screen cell D11.

Look at the formulas in cells E11 through G11.

Each of these formulas works the same way. You should be able to see how the computer calculates the numbers shown in the screen cells.

13. Suppose file cell D15 contains the formula 8*7. What will appear in screen cell D15?

14. What does the formula +C15*E2 tell the computer to do?

▪ Two Kinds of Formulas

You have seen two different kinds of formulas for calculating the numbers in the multiplication table. The first kind showed the actual numbers to be multiplied. The second kind told the computer where to get the numbers to multiply together. Both of these methods give the right answer. Which method is better? Let us see.

Go to cell A11. Keep your eye on the last row of the table as you change 9 to 20.

By changing only the number in cell A11, you changed one whole row of products correctly. Let us try this again.

Go to cell A7. Change 5 to 20.

This time, some of the products in the row are correct. However, the first two numbers did not change at all.

Look again at the formulas in cells C7 and D7.

Now you see why the numbers in those screen cells did not change. The formula 5*5 will always produce 25.

Now look at cell E7.

The formula here is +A7*E5. The number in A7 is 20, and the number in E5 is 7. The computer calculated the correct product, which is 140. The errors in the first row would not have happened if the formulas had used cell names rather than simple numbers.

Give the Zoom command to look at formulas for the whole table.

Some formulas use cell names. These formulas will give correct results when you change the numbers at the side of the table. Four of the formulas contain numbers, not cell names. These formulas will produce the same results no matter what changes you make elsewhere.

Give the Zoom command again. Move to cell C7 and change the formula to +A7*C5.

Now you see the correct value, 100, in screen cell C7. The plus sign at the beginning of the formula is important. If you left the plus sign out, the computer would assume that you were entering a label that began with the letter A. Any time you enter a *formula that begins with a letter,* type a plus sign first.

Change the formula for cell D7 to +A7*D5.

Now the whole row is correct.

Change 20 to 15 in cell A7.

All the formulas in the top row are working correctly now. Some of the cells in the second row still refer to numbers rather than cell names.

This session introduced you to all the important features of the spreadsheet program in AppleWorks. The most important of these is the ability to write formulas that refer to cell locations. If you have time, do some of the "On Your Own" activities below. Then quit the computer as usual.

15. Suppose cell A1 contains the value 10. Cell A2 contains the formula +A1+5. Cell A3 contains the formula +A2*2. What appears in screen cells A1, A2, and A3?

16. Suppose a formula begins with a cell name. What must you type to tell the computer you are not entering a label?

If you have time:

ON YOUR OWN

- The file Multiply should be on the REVIEW/ADD/CHANGE screen. In cells C8 and D8, change the formulas to new ones that use cell names rather than numbers. Change values in column A and make sure the formulas are working correctly. Change values in row 5. Use the Name command (⌖ N) to change the name of the file to NewTable. Save the file.

- Clear the Desktop. Add the file Muffins. Explore the cells. Look for values and labels. See which values are numbers and which are formulas. Change numbers and see what happens to the numbers that are calculated by formulas. When you finish, remove the file from the Desktop and throw out your changes.

- Add a new spreadsheet file to the Desktop (from scratch). In rows 5 to 14 of column B, enter the numbers 1 through 10. In the same rows of column C, enter formulas that will calculate the squares of each number in column B. The formulas should use cell names. Be sure to start each formula with a plus sign. When everything is working, change the numbers in column B and watch the changes in column C.

Spreadsheet Files

SESSION GOALS: • Review the parts of a spreadsheet file and the movement of the cell cursor.
• Understand the difference between labels and values.
• Understand the first-key rule for entering information into a spreadsheet file.
• Understand the difference between file cells and screen cells.
• Understand the importance of using cell names in formulas.
• Be aware of the similarities between writing a program and creating a spreadsheet.

▪ The Parts of a Spreadsheet

The word "spreadsheet" existed long before there were computers. A spreadsheet is a large sheet of paper with lines that divide it into rows and columns. People use spreadsheets to work with lists and tables of numbers. This is especially true when some numbers have to be calculated from other numbers on the spreadsheet.

The spreadsheet program   In Session 12, you began exploring the *spreadsheet program* in AppleWorks. This program does three main things. First, it helps you with the task of entering and changing spreadsheet information. Second, it automatically does all the calculations you ask for. Third, it displays the results on the screen or prints the results on paper.

Screen appearance   The computer's spreadsheet is divided into rows and columns. The rows are numbered from the top down. The columns are identified by letters in alphabetical order from left to right. These rows and columns divide the spreadsheet into *cells*. The computer displays information in the cells. The *cell name* tells you which column and row contain the cell. For example, cell B5 is the cell in column B and row 5.

Dimensions   In AppleWorks spreadsheet files, you may have up to 999 rows and 127 columns. This is a total of 126,873 cells. Most applications use only a small number of these cells. (This is a good thing, because the computer would run out of memory long before you filled all possible cells with information.)

The cell cursor   To move the cell cursor through the computer spreadsheet, you used most of the same commands learned earlier for moving through a word processor or data base file. This time, however, the commands operate on the *cell cursor*. This large rectangle highlights the entire cell it is moved to. The ⬅ and ➡ keys move the cell cursor horizontally. (So do TAB and ⌂ | TAB .) The ↑ and ↓ keys move the cell cursor vertically. The ⌂ key magnifies the effect of the arrow keys.

Scrolling   As with word processor files and data base files, you can also scroll up and down through a spreadsheet file. In addition, you can scroll left and right, bringing new columns into view as old ones disappear. In AppleWorks, this *horizontal scrolling* is available *only* with spreadsheet files.

The cell indicator   At the left and below the dashed line at the bottom of the screen, there is an area called the *cell indicator*. This area always shows the name of whatever cell contains the cursor. If the cell is blank, only the name appears in the cell indicator. Otherwise, the type of information and the actual information in that cell are seen. In effect, the cell indicator is a peek into the spreadsheet file itself.

▪ Information in a Spreadsheet

A spreadsheet file can contain only two types of information. When you enter new information into any spreadsheet, you must be aware of what kind it is.

Values   Most of the information in spreadsheet files is called *value* information. A value is either a number or a formula that tells the computer to calculate a number. Wherever a value is stored in a spreadsheet file, you will see a number on the screen in the same cell.

Labels   The other kind of information in a spreadsheet file is a *label*. Labels are usually words or phrases that act as column row headings or other descriptions of the numbers in a spreadsheet. A label is any set of letters, numbers, or other symbols that you do *not* want the computer to treat as a value.

Formulas   A *formula* is a special kind of value. It tells the computer to do calculations with numbers. For example, if cell $G7$ in the *file* contains the formula $2*F7$, this tells the computer to double whatever value is shown in cell $F7$. The computer then displays the resulting number on the *screen* in cell $G7$.

▪ Entering Information

You enter information into a spreadsheet file in two steps. First, you position the cursor at the cell where the information is to go. Then you type the new information. You can erase typing errors with the DELETE key. If you change your mind and decide not to enter new information, a tap of the ESC key will restore whatever old information was in the cell. Otherwise, when you tap the RETURN key, your entry becomes part of the spreadsheet file.

First-key rule   Suppose that you are about to enter new information into a cell. The first key you tap tells the computer what type of information to expect. If you tap a letter key, the computer automatically assumes you want to enter a label. If you tap a number key, the computer assumes you want to enter a value. This is called the *first-key rule*. (A plus sign, minus sign, left parenthesis, or at sign, @, also signals a value.)

Entering numbers as labels   If you want to enter a label that begins with anything but a letter, such as a number or a space, you need to take special action. You begin by typing a quotation mark. The quotation mark does not become part of the label. Do *not*, however, use a matching quotation mark to finish the label. If you do, it *will* become part of the label.

Entering a cell name as a value   The first-key rule causes trouble when you want to enter a formula that begins with a cell name. If you just start typing, the first letter of the cell name tells the computer you are entering a label. But you want to enter a value. The solution is to start by typing a plus sign. (If you forget to do this, just tap (ESC) and start over.)

▪ The Two Versions of a Spreadsheet

The computer keeps track of two different versions of every spreadsheet. One version is the spreadsheet file itself. The other is the version you normally see on the screen. The two versions are much alike—but there are important differences.

File cells and screen cells   Each cell in a computer spreadsheet exists in two versions. We will call one the *file cell* and the other the *screen cell*. Sometimes the file cell and the screen cell contain exactly the same thing. For example, if file cell C9 contains the label Price, then you normally see Price on the screen in cell C9. But this is not always true. If file cell D3 contains the formula 2*3, then screen cell D3 normally will contain 6.

Seeing the file cells   There are two ways to see the information actually stored in a file cell. The first is to look at the cell indicator for that cell. If the file cell contains a formula, you will see it in the cell indicator—and *only* there. The second way is to use the Zoom command. This command lets you see all the file cells at once on the screen; the screen cells disappear. Zoom again, and you switch back to the screen cells.

The spreadsheet file   When you create a new spreadsheet, you put information into file cells. When you edit a spreadsheet, you change information in file cells. When you save a spreadsheet on your disk, you save all the file cells. In short, a spreadsheet file contains only the information in the file cells, not the screen cells.

The screen   The information on the screen is a *result* of the data and formulas stored in all the file cells. Unless you use the Zoom command, the screen shows the *output* coming from the information in the file cells.

Cause and effect   The best way to think about these important differences in cells is in terms of cause and effect. The information in a file cell is the cause. The information in the corresponding screen cell is the effect. A formula in a file cell causes the computer to calculate a number and display it in the corresponding screen cell. The only way to change what you see on the screen is to change information in one or more file cells. In other words, *you* control the file cells, and *they* control the screen cells.

▪ The Power of Formulas

The ability to put a formula into a spreadsheet cell is what makes the computer spreadsheet so much more useful than a regular paper spreadsheet. In fact, without formulas, you might as well use a word processor program to create and edit tables of numbers and labels.

A calculator in every cell   In many ways, working with a spreadsheet program is like having a pocket calculator in every cell of the spreadsheet. When you put a formula into a file cell, you usually tell the computer to add, subtract, multiply, or divide numbers. These are the same things you do with a pocket calculator. The spreadsheet calculator allows you to do these four standard arithmetic operations and many others.

A calculator with memory   Some pocket calculators come with one or two memory cells in which numbers can be stored. Later in a calculation, you can get the number back by keying the memory cell. The spreadsheet calculator has thousands of memory cells. Every spreadsheet screen cell is also a memory cell. You can use the number in the screen cell just by writing the cell name into a formula. Thus, if screen cell F7 contains the number 23795.41, the formula 2*F7 has exactly the same effect as the formula 2*23795.41.

The advantage of using cell names   Whenever possible, you should use cell names instead of numbers in your spreadsheet formulas. If you do so, when you change a number in one part of the spreadsheet, the computer will automatically change all the other numbers that depend upon that number.

An example   Suppose a hardware store manager wants a spreadsheet to keep track of the items sold each week. After the name of each item, one spreadsheet cell shows the selling price, one cell shows the number of items sold that week, and the last cell shows the total amount of money received for that item. For example, here is how row 9 in that spreadsheet might look:

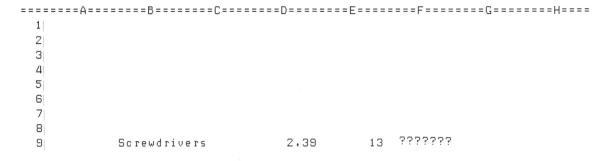

```
========A========B========C========D========E========F========G========H====
1|
2|
3|
4|
5|
6|
7|
8|
9|        Screwdrivers               2.39        13  ???????
```

Numbers or cell names? Cell F9 has question marks because the store manager is not certain what should be written. There are two possibilities. The formula 2.39*13 tells the computer to multiply the unit price, $2.39, times the number of units sold, 13. Another formula, +D9*E9, would give the same answer. Which formula is better?

Cell names make changes easy A formula with cell names is almost always better than one that uses only numbers. In this example, the formula +D9*E9 says to multiply *whatever* numbers are in screen cells D9 and E9 and display the result. If you later discover that 15, not 13, screwdrivers were sold, then all you need to do is change the number in cell E9. The number in screen cell F9 is corrected automatically because the formula refers to cell name E9.

Reusing a spreadsheet If you use cell names in all your spreadsheet formulas, then you will find that the same spreadsheet can be used again and again. In the example here, the hardware store manager could use last week's spreadsheet as the starting point for this week's spreadsheet. Most of the changes would go in column E, the number of units sold. A few prices might also change in column D. Once those changes are made, the old spreadsheet becomes the new one. By printing the spreadsheet, the manager has a report of the week's sales totals for each item.

▪ Programming Concepts

If you already know a little bit about writing programs for a computer, spreadsheets will be easy to understand. In this section, you will see the connection.

Data types A spreadsheet program allows you to work with two different types of information: *labels* and *values*. The same is true of computer languages, such as BASIC. BASIC uses different words. A *string* in BASIC is the same thing as a *label* in a spreadsheet. *Numeric data items* in BASIC are the same as *values* in a spreadsheet.

Formulas and expressions A spreadsheet formula is the same thing as a numeric expression in programming. In BASIC, for example, you can write this statement:

```
LET X = 23 * 5 + 37
```

The information to the right of the equal sign is an example of a numeric expression. It tells the computer to multiply the first two numbers and then add the result to the third number. The same expression, 23*5+37, can be entered as a spreadsheet formula. The expression gives the same result both in a spreadsheet and in a program line.

Cell names and variables The term *cell name* in a spreadsheet means the same thing as the term *variable* in programming. Again, in BASIC, you can write a statement such as PRINT B3 * A2. In programming, B3 and A2 are names of variables. These names stand for places in the computer's memory. The above statement tells the computer to find the numbers in locations B3 and A2, multiply them, and print the result. With a spreadsheet program, you get the same effect by putting the formula +B3*A2 in a cell.

Programs and spreadsheets The terms *computer program* and *spreadsheet file* also mean something similar. A spreadsheet file, after all, is nothing but a collection of labels, numbers, and formulas. The formulas are instructions to the computer to perform calculations and display results on the screen. You can even think of the labels as instructions: They tell the computer simply to display the label at the right place on the screen.

Output Each *file cell* of a spreadsheet contains your instructions to the computer. These instructions tell the computer what to display in the corresponding *screen cell*. In other words, a file cell functions in the same way as an output statement, such as the Print statement in BASIC. In any programming situation, it is important to know which information on the screen is the *program* and which is the *output* of the program.

Running the program When you write a computer program, you first enter the statements. Then you make changes. When you want to see the output, you give a command to run the program. With a spreadsheet, you simply make a change in one of your file cells. As soon as the change is complete, the computer automatically recalculates the formulas and displays any new output.

Programming ideas In all the above ways, working with a spreadsheet file is like writing, editing, and running a program. The main ideas are the same. In both cases, you give instructions to the computer. The computer carries out the instructions and displays the results. If you are familiar with programming ideas, you know many basic things about spreadsheets and will find them easier to understand.

QUESTIONS

1. What are the three main things a spreadsheet program does?
2. Where is spreadsheet cell D13 located? Where is cell AB56 located?
3. What does horizontal scrolling mean?
4. What information is always shown in the cell indicator?
5. Is it possible to enter a number as a label in a file cell? If so, how? If not, why not?
6. Suppose a formula begins with a cell name. What should you type to tell the computer that you want to enter a value, not a label?
7. What kind of information in a file cell causes the same information to appear in the screen cell? Give an example.
8. What kind of information in a file cell causes different information to appear in the screen cell? Give an example.
9. What are two ways to see what information is contained in a given file cell?
10. Why is each cell in a spreadsheet like a pocket calculator?
11. Some pocket calculators have memory. What parts of a computer spreadsheet are like the calculator's memory?
12. If you want to create a spreadsheet that can be used again and again with new data, how should you write the formulas you need?
13. In terms of programming languages, what type of data is a spreadsheet label? a spreadsheet value?
14. What part of a computer spreadsheet is like a computer program? What part is the output of the program?
15. What part of a computer spreadsheet is like a variable in a computer program?

More Spreadsheet Tools

SESSION GOALS: • Enter a number as a spreadsheet label.
• Use functions in spreadsheet formulas.
• Copy formulas from one spreadsheet cell to another.
• Save a spreadsheet file and print it.
• Insert and delete rows in a spreadsheet file.

▪ Finding Formulas in Spreadsheets

In your last session at the computer, you learned the main tools for creating and using any spreadsheet file. In this session you will explore three new spreadsheets.

Start the computer with AppleWorks in the usual way.

Add the file BowlingScores **to the Desktop.**

Take a few minutes to read the information on the screen.

This spreadsheet shows a summary of the scores for a team of five bowlers over a five-week period. The column at the right shows each bowler's average score after five weeks. The row at the bottom shows the sum of the team scores each week. The lower right entry shows the sum of the averages.

Move the cursor to cell A6 **and look at the cell indicator.**

Cell A6 contains a label. It is part of the name Mary Azevedo. The rest of the name is in cell B6.

Move the cursor to cell C8.

This cell contains the value, 42, Susan Roth's score in week one. Suppose that her score was entered incorrectly. Instead of the score 42, her correct score was 242.

Jot down the team total for week one and the five-week average for Roth.

These two numbers should depend on Roth's score. If you change her score, these two numbers should also change. See whether they do.

Type 242 **and tap** (RETURN).

The team total went up by 200 points, and Roth's average went up by 40 points. This tells you that your spreadsheet file contains formulas that use cell names.

1. If you change a value in one file cell and you see a change in the value of a different screen cell, what does this tell you?
2. Suppose file cell G15 contains the formula +A1*A1. If screen cell A1 contains the value 5, what will appear in screen cell G15? If you change the value in screen cell A1 to 10, what will happen in screen cell G15?

▪ Functions in Formulas

Some of the numbers in the screen cells are there because of formulas in the file cells. Let us take a closer look at these formulas.

Move the cursor to cell C10. Read the formula in the cell indicator.

This is much like the formulas you saw in Session 12. It tells the computer to add the five numbers from cells C4 through C8. The spreadsheet program gives you another way to do sums.

Look at the formula in file cell D10.

This formula also tells the computer to add five numbers together. It uses a **function** and a **range** of cells. The function name is @SUM. The range is D4..D8. The function indicates what the computer is supposed to do. Function names always begin with the symbol @. The range tells which cells to act upon. In this case, the function tells the computer to sum the cells from D4 through D8.

Look at the formulas in file cells E10 and F10.

These formulas also use the @SUM function.

Look at the formula in file cell H4.

This formula tells the computer to sum the numbers from cells C4 through G4. Then the computer divides the sum by 5. In other words, the computer computes the average of Tom Jones's bowling scores. As you know, there is another way to compute a sum.

Look at the formula in file cell H5.

The @SUM function works the same way here as before. But this time the range is a row rather than a column of cells. There is still another way to compute an average.

Look at the formula in file cell H6.

There is a new function in this formula. Function @COUNT tells how many cells in a given range contain values. It does not count cells with labels or empty cells. In this example, there are seven cells in the range, but only five contain values.

Look at the formula in file cell H7.

This is the last, and by far the easiest way to compute an average. The @AVG function sums the values in a given range, counts the values, and then divides by the number of values counted.

3. A file cell contains the formula @SUM(G4..G10). What does this tell the computer to do?

4. Suppose a range of cells contains two labels, three blanks, and five values. What number does the @COUNT function give for this range?

▪ Copying Formulas

In most spreadsheets, the same formula, with few changes, appears in many different file cells. You can, of course, type each formula in each cell. To save time and work, the spreadsheet program gives you a tool for making copies of a formula.

Clear the file BowlingScores **from the Desktop. Throw out changes.**

Add the file Muffins **to the Desktop.**

This spreadsheet shows a recipe for whole wheat muffins. Column D shows the amounts of ingredients needed to make 12 muffins. Column E shows the amounts of ingredients for 24 muffins.

See what kind of information is stored in file cells D6 **through** D12.

Each of these file cells contains a number.

Put the cursor in cell E12.

This file cell contains a formula instead of a number. The formula says to double the amount in cell D12. This is correct, since you need twice as much milk when there are twice as many muffins.

Look at the rest of the formulas in column E.

Each formula says to double the amount for each ingredient. All seven formulas are similar. Once you have written one of the formulas, there should be an easy way to have the computer create all the rest. There is. To see how this works, suppose you wanted to expand the spreadsheet to calculate recipe amounts for 36, 48, 60, and 72 muffins. First, you will need some new headings.

Put the cursor at cell E3.

You need copies of the label in this cell in cells F3 through I3.

Give the Copy command ⌘ C **. Tap** (RETURN) **to say that you want to copy within the worksheet.**

The computer is waiting for you to select more than one cell to be copied. You want to copy only one cell.

Tap (RETURN).

The computer is waiting for you to move the cursor to the first cell where you want the copy to appear.

Move the cursor to cell F3. **Type a period.**

The period tells the computer you are going to highlight more than one cell. Now the computer is waiting for you to move the cursor to the last cell where you want the copy to appear.

Move the cursor to cell I3 **and tap** (RETURN).

That is all there is to it. You have put a copy of the label in cell E3 into cells F3 through I3.

Move the cursor to cell E5. **Give the Copy command.**

Use the method you just learned to put a copy of this label into cells F5 **through** I5.

Put the numbers 36, 48, 60, and 72 in the proper places in row 4 of the spreadsheet.

Now comes the interesting part. The Copy command also works with formulas but a little differently.

Put the cursor at cell F6.

To make 36 muffins, you need three times as much of everything instead of twice as much.

Enter the formula 3*D6 **in file cell** F6.

The spreadsheet cell now says that you need 6 cups of wheat flour to make 36 muffins. The formula is okay. Now you need similar formulas in cells F7 through F12. Try using the Copy command.

With the cursor in cell F6, **give the command** ⌘ C **. Then tap** (RETURN).

Tap (RETURN) **since you want to copy only the cell** F6.

Tap the ↓ **key to go to the first cell where you want a copy of the formula. Then type a period.**

Move the cursor down to cell F12. **Then tap** (RETURN).

There is a mysterious prompt at the bottom of the screen. It highlights D6 in the formula 3*D6. Then the computer asks whether you want cell name D6 to have No change or to have a Relative change.

Tap Return **to say that you want no change.**

Whoops! That will not make very good muffins.

Look at the formulas in file cells F7 **through** F12.

Now you can see what is wrong. The formulas are exactly the same. They all refer to cell D6.

Look at the formulas in file cells E6 **through** E12.

These formulas are *similar* but not the *same*. The option you should have used in the last step of the copy process was Relative. Let us try the copy process again.

Put the cursor in cell F6 **and give the Copy command. Then tap** (RETURN).

Tap (RETURN) **to select cell** F6. **Move the cursor down to cell** F7 **and type a period.**

Move the cursor down to cell F12 **and tap** (RETURN).

This time select Relative **and tap** (RETURN).

Success. Now the formulas are all correct. Each quantity for making 36 is three times the quantity for making 12. The Relative option adjusts the formula as it moves it from the original cell to each new cell. Now you should be able to fill out the rest of the table.

Move to cell G6 **and enter the formula** 4*D6. **Then use the Copy command with the** Relative **option to put copies in cells** G7 **through** G13.

Use the same process to complete the last two columns in the table.

5. Suppose there is a label in cell B5. You want to copy this label into five other cells. What are the first two steps you must take?
6. Suppose cell D8 contains the formula 3+D7. You want to move a copy of the formula into cell E8. If you use the No change mode, what will the new formula be? What if you use the Relative mode?

▪ Saving and Printing the Spreadsheet

The spreadsheet you have been working with is more useful now. This is a good time to save your work and print a copy of it if you have a printer.

Go to the Main Menu and give the Save Desktop **command. When prompted, give the** current disk **command.**

Give command number 2 to save the file with a different name.

Give command ⌘Y to delete the old name. Type the name Recipe **and tap** (RETURN).

That does it. The new version of the spreadsheet file is now saved with the name Recipe. The next step is to print it. (If you do not have a printer connected to your computer, you will have to take your Computer Applications DATA Disk to a computer with a printer.)

With the file Recipe **on the REVIEW/ADD/CHANGE screen, give the Print command ⌘P. Insert the AppleWorks Program Disk when prompted.**

You have four options. You can print all the cells in the spreadsheet, a group of rows, a group of columns, or any rectangular block. Print the whole table.

Tap (RETURN) **to choose** All.

Make certain the printer is on and ready to receive information.

Select the printer model and tap (RETURN).

Type today's date and tap (RETURN).

Tap (RETURN) **for one copy.**

Printing should begin at once. The computer sends a copy of the spreadsheet to the printer. Printing begins at row 1 and ends with the last row that contains any information.

7. A spreadsheet file can contain up to 999 rows. How many rows will be sent to the printer if you select All after giving the Print command?

8. On which screen must you be to give the Print command?

▪ Inserting and Deleting Rows

Sometimes you need to add whole new rows in the middle of a spreadsheet. You also may need to delete rows. AppleWorks has simple tools for inserting and deleting both rows and columns.

Clear the Desktop. Duplicate a copy of the file Groceries **from your Computer Applications DATA Disk to the Desktop.**

Here is the beginning of a spreadsheet for a weekly grocery list. To convert this spreadsheet into one for your family, changes are needed. You will want to delete some of the items, add new items, and change some of the numbers. Before doing that, let us explore the cells in the spreadsheet.

Start at cell C6. Look at the cell indicator as you move the cursor across the row.

This row contains labels, numerical values, and a formula. The cost in column G is calculated from the two numbers to the left.

Move the cursor down through column G.

The formulas in these file cells are all similar.

Give the ⌖9 command.

This takes you to the last row with information in it.

Give the ⌖1 command.

As expected, this takes you to the top row. You should now have a good idea of the shape of this spreadsheet file. To add and delete information, you will need some new tools. For example, suppose you want to add two new meat items to the list. You need some blank rows for that.

Place the cursor anywhere in row 7. Give the Insert command ⌖I.

The computer asks whether you want to insert rows or columns.

Tap RETURN to choose Rows.

Type 2 and tap RETURN to insert two blank rows.

You have now inserted two blank rows into the spreadsheet. You can use these rows to enter new information. You can delete rows in the same way. Here is how to delete the two rows you entered, as well as the Chicken row:

With the cursor still on row 7, give the Delete command ⌖D. Choose Rows.

Tap the ↓ arrow key twice.

Now three rows in the spreadsheet are highlighted.

Tap RETURN.

That is all there is to it. The three rows are now gone from the spreadsheet file.

This brings you to the end of your work with the spreadsheet program. If you have time, try some of the On Your Own activities. When you have finished, quit the computer in the usual way.

9. Suppose you put the cursor in row 9 and then you insert two blank rows. What happens to the original cells in row 9?

10. Suppose you delete row 5 in a spreadsheet file. What happens to the information stored in the file cells in that row?

- If necessary, put the spreadsheet file Groceries on the Desktop. Change any prices or quantities you want. Delete any rows that contain items not on your family's shopping list. Insert rows and add new items that are on your list. When you are finished, save the file with the new name MyList. Print a copy of your list.

- Put the file MyList on the Desktop. Insert a new row just below the last row in Meats. At the right end of the new row, enter a formula that adds all the prices in the last column of Meats. This will give you a subtotal that tells you how much you are spending for meat. Add other rows to compute subtotals for the other kinds of food in the table. At the bottom of the table, write a formula that adds all the subtotals together. Put a label beside it that says Grand Total. Save the file.

- Put the spreadsheet file Muffins on the Desktop. Put the cursor at cell E9. Read the formula in the cell indicator. Insert two blank rows. The information that used to be in row 9 is now in row 11. Move the cursor to cell E11 and look at the formula again. Explain what happened to the formula when it was moved from E9 to E11.

Using Spreadsheets

SESSION GOALS:
- Review functions in spreadsheet formulas.
- Review the steps for copying cells.
- Understand the meaning of relative copying.
- Review the steps necessary to print a spreadsheet.
- Learn ways in which spreadsheets are valuable.

▪ Functions in Spreadsheet Formulas

The main advantage of computer spreadsheets is that the numbers in some cells can be calculated automatically from numbers in other cells. As we said earlier, you can think of a spreadsheet as having a calculator in each cell. You can program each of these calculators to do whatever arithmetic you want. The formula you enter into a spreadsheet file cell is the program, or set of instructions, that tells the computer what calculation to perform. The result appears in the corresponding screen cell.

Adding numbers In Session 14, one of the file cells in spreadsheet BowlingScores contained this long formula:

    +C4+C5+C6+C7+C8

This formula is an instruction to the computer. The formula says two things: First, add the numbers in screen cells C4 through C8; second, display the result. The formula is in file cell C10, so the result appears in screen cell C10.

Functions in formulas In Session 14, you saw a different formula for doing a similar task. File cell D10 also tells the computer to add numbers in five cells and display the result. However, the formula in D10 is very different from the one in C10. The one in D10 is this:

    @SUM(D4...D8)

This is an example of a *function*. The name of the function is @SUM. The symbols D4...D8 stand for a *range* of five screen cells in column D. The function tells the computer to sum the numbers in those cells.

Other functions You also saw other formulas that used the functions @COUNT and @AVG. The spreadsheet program allows you to use many different functions in your formulas. Each function tells the computer to perform some particular task on one or more pieces of data. The instructions to carry out each task are part of the spreadsheet program in AppleWorks. Functions often make formulas easier to write and understand.

▪ How Functions Work

A *function name* is an abbreviation that stands for a calculation. When you enter a function name into a spreadsheet cell, you are telling the computer to perform that calculation on the values in cells you specify or on values you supply. In AppleWorks and most other spreadsheet programs, all function names start with the @ symbol. Following the function name, you supply the data you want the function to work on. This data must be enclosed in parentheses. For example, suppose file cell G1 contains the formula

```
@SUM(A1...A10)
```

@SUM means "add up the values in the following cells." A1...A10 means "cells A1 through A10." After doing the sum, the computer puts the result into screen cell G1.

Functions and values Some functions work on a single value, either a value in a cell or one that you supply. @SQRT, the square-root function, is one of these. The result of @SQRT(25) is 5. The result of @SQRT(F13) is the square root of the number appearing in screen cell F13.

Functions and ranges The functions @SUM, @COUNT, and @AVG, which you saw in Session 14, work on ranges of cells. A range is a row, column, or block of cells. You write the range by naming the first and last cell. The two cell names are separated by periods.

Example of ranges The range C5...C9 means the cells C5, C6, C7, C8, and C9 in column C. Likewise, the range B3...G3 means the cells B3, C3, D3, E3, F3, and G3 in row 3. @AVG(F30...G34) tells the computer to calculate the average of the 10 values in the block range F30...G34.

Empty cells and cells with labels It sometimes happens that a range of cells will include some that are empty or have labels instead of values. This usually causes no problems. For most functions, empty cells and cells with labels are ignored. For example, the function @SUM(G1...G999) causes only the numbers that appear anywhere in column G to be summed. Anything else in column G is ignored.

A user trap Watch out for this problem: You write a formula such as 2*H3. By accident, H3 contains a label or is blank. In a programming language, this leads to a "type mismatch" error message. In spreadsheet programs, however, no error is reported. Instead, the computer uses the value zero for a blank screen cell and for one that contains a label. This can lead to surprising results.

▪ Functions and Lists

Some functions work on **a lists of cells**, such as @SUM(G3,H4,M7). This function tells the computer to add the numbers in screen cells G3,

H4, and M7. The list in this example is just the three cell names. A comma must separate items in any list.

List of ranges The list in the paragraph above is a list of individual cell names. You can also have a **list of ranges**. Suppose you wanted to find the largest number in the row of cells A1 through G1 or in the column of cells B1 through B10. The function @MAX(A1...G1, B1...B10) would do the job. The list here has two ranges. As usual, a comma separates the two items in the list.

List The term "list" stands for one or more items, each separated from the next by a comma. An item can be either a single cell name or a range of cells. Many powerful spreadsheet functions allow you to do calculations on whatever list you write in parentheses after the function name.

AppleWorks functions Here is a short table of AppleWorks functions for use in spreadsheet formulas. You can read about other functions in the AppleWorks reference manual. The term "value" means either a number or a cell name. The term "list" is defined in the preceding paragraph.

Function	Result
@ABS(*value*)	Absolute value of the value
@AVG(*list*)	Average of the values in the list
@COUNT(*list*)	Number of values in the list
@INT(*value*)	Integer part of the value
@MAX(*list*)	The largest value in the list
@MIN(*list*)	The smallest value in the list
@SQRT(*value*)	Square root of the value
@SUM(*list*)	The sum of all values in the list

Functions in programming If you are familiar with programming, you already know about functions. For example, the INT and SQR functions in BASIC are like the INT and SQRT functions in AppleWorks. As in programming, one or more values must be *passed into* a spreadsheet function, and exactly one value is *returned* by the function. The function tells the computer how to process the values passed to it. The value of the function is the result that comes back from the processing. These ideas are the same whether you are working with a spreadsheet or a computer program.

▪ Copying Labels and Numbers

In Session 14, you learned commands for making a copy of a label in one cell and putting the copy in other cells. You can copy numbers from cell to cell in the same way.

The Copy command As with the word processor and the data base programs in AppleWorks, the Copy command ⎕ⓒ⎕ is the starting point. You first move the cursor to the cell with the label or value you want to copy. Then you give the Copy command.

Selecting the cells to copy After you give the Copy command, the computer prompts you to select additional cells to copy. You can copy a single cell or several cells at once. For example, if a label took up three cells, you could move a copy of the whole label by selecting all three cells at this time. You make the selection by using the arrow keys to highlight the cells. When your selection is complete, you tap ⎕RETURN⎕.

Selecting the destination Next, the computer prompts you to select all cells in which you want the copy to appear. Again, you use the arrow keys to highlight these destination cells. Finally, you tap ⎕RETURN⎕ and see the copies appear in the highlighted cells. Unlike the Copy command for the word processor, the copy command for the spreadsheet writes over any information there may have been at the destination.

▪ Copying Formulas in Spreadsheet Files

In Session 14, you also learned how to copy a formula in one file cell into a group of other file cells. Cell formulas are at the heart of most spreadsheet operations. All spreadsheet programs give you a tool for making copies of a formula.

Similar formulas Quite often, you will see groups of formulas in spreadsheets that look almost the same. The operations are identical, but the cell names are different. For example, cell D9 might contain the formula 2*B9, and cell D10 might contain the formula 2*B10. The two formulas are different, but they differ in a simple way. Spreadsheet programs have a tool for dealing with this difference when you copy a formula from cell to cell.

The Copy command The process of copying formulas is almost the same as that for copying numbers and labels. However, there is one extra step you must go through whenever a formula contains a cell name. Just before putting the copy of the formula into the destination cells, the computer asks you what you want done with each cell name in the formula. You can ask for No change, or else you can ask for a change that is Relative.

No change mode If you ask for no change, the computer leaves that cell name exactly as it is when moving the copy to another cell. You might want to do this if the same number is needed in many different formulas. For example, if you were setting up a spreadsheet to show the interest you earn on a bank account, you might put the interest rate in one cell. Then all formulas that needed the interest rate would use that cell name. (That way you could easily change the interest rate later without having to rewrite your formulas.) If you copied one of those formulas from one cell to another, you would *not* want the cell name to change.

Relative mode The relative mode means that the cell name *should* change when you move the formula to another cell. Suppose the formula you are copying is one that means "triple the number two cells to my left." If the formula is in cell D9, then the formula is 3*B9. Why? The answer is because cell B9 is two cells to the left of D9 in the ninth row. Now, suppose you want to put a copy of the formula in cells D10 through D30, but you still want it to mean "triple the number two cells to my left." You want the formulas to be 3*B10, 3*B11, 3*B12, and so on, up to 3*B30. In this case, you *do* want the cell name to be changed when the formula is copied.

Name shifting If you choose the relative option for a cell name in a formula, the kind of change just described happens automatically when you copy the formula. If you move the copy down five rows, the row number in the new cell name will be five greater than the row number in the original cell name. In other words, the name of the cell is shifted as it is moved.

What it means There is an easy way to think about relative changes in a cell name. Just think of the formula in terms of the words "left," "right," "above," and "below." Here is an example. Suppose you see this formula in cell F3:

    +E3+G3+F2+F4

Instead of thinking about these cells by their names, think about their positions *relative to the cell with the formula*. With a little thought, you can see that the formula really says this:

    left + right + above + below

Now, suppose you copy the formula from F3 into cell B7. If you choose the relative mode for each one of the four cell names, the new formula will be:

    +A7+C7+B6+B8

However, the new formula will still say to add the numbers in the cells to the left, right, above, and below the cell with the formula. The formula has changed, but the meaning is the same. That is the whole idea of relative copying.

▪ Printing Spreadsheets

As long as you work with a spreadsheet on the computer, you are the only one who can see the information as it develops. Sooner or later, however, you will want a paper copy that can be reproduced and made available to others.

The Print command   As with the other application programs in AppleWorks, printing a spreadsheet begins with the Print command (⌘P). Your spreadsheet file must be visible on the REVIEW/ADD/CHANGE screen before you give the command.

Options   The computer prompts you to say how much of the spreadsheet you want printed. You can choose all of it, a block of rows, a block of columns, or a rectangular block of cells. If you select rows, columns, or blocks, the computer asks you to highlight the screen cells you want printed.

Output to the printer   After choosing the cells to print, you select the printer model, enter a date, and say how many copies you want. After that, the computer begins printing your screen cells on paper. If the output has too many columns to fit on a single page, the computer divides it and prints one group of columns at a time.

▪ Inserting and Deleting Rows and Columns

When you create a new spreadsheet, you often discover that you have left something out. If the information can go at the end of the table, you simply move the cell cursor there and start typing. But what if you need to insert a whole row or column into the middle of the table?

The Insert command   To insert a new blank row, you first move the cursor to any cell on the row in which you want the blank row to appear. Then you give the Insert command (⌘I). The computer asks whether you want to insert rows or columns. When you choose rows, it asks how many to insert. As soon as you enter a number, the computer inserts the new rows, moving the others down. Column insertion works the same.

The Delete command   Deleting rows or columns begins the same way. You move the cursor to any cell in the row or column to be deleted. Then you give the Delete command (⌘D) and choose to delete either rows or columns. The next step is to highlight the rows or columns you want removed. When you tap (RETURN), the rows or columns disappear permanently from the spreadsheet file on the Desktop.

Relative changes in formulas   If you insert a row or column, the computer automatically makes a *relative* change in all formulas affected by the change. After the insertion, some formulas are changed, but they still have their old meanings. The same is true after a deletion. This is almost always what you want to happen.

▪ Spreadsheet Applications

These four sessions have introduced you to the main ideas you need to make spreadsheets of your own. Most other spreadsheet programs are very much like AppleWorks, so you should have an easy time with them.

What-if questions The power of the spreadsheet programs comes from formulas. If a dozen formulas use the cell name C3, then a change in the number in C3 will cause a dozen other numbers to change at the same time. If C3 contains the interest rate at your bank, for example, the formulas could show how much money you will earn each month for a year. Now you can play what-if games. What if the interest rate changes? How much would you earn? To answer the question, all you have to do is change the number in cell C3. The 12 monthly earnings automatically change, and you see the effect.

Financial planning The above example is a simple case of **financial modeling**. Many businesses use spreadsheet files to help them plan their income and expenses for the coming months or years. This type of file would contain estimates of things such as raw material prices, labor costs, production rates, selling prices, and units sold. The file would also contain many formulas for calculating separate costs, subtotals, and grand totals. With such a spreadsheet file, a business manager can see how the business will be affected by day-to-day decisions about prices and costs.

Tax tables Spreadsheet programs are also useful for preparing income tax forms. These forms are just rows and columns of labels and numbers. Furthermore, many numbers on a tax form must be computed from other numbers. Some blanks on a form contain subtotals. Other blanks on a form have space for a number that appeared on another form. This is an ideal job for a spreadsheet program.

Other applications All spreadsheet problems are number problems. Whenever you find that you are writing columns of numbers on paper and doing arithmetic with them, you can probably use a spreadsheet program to make the job easier. Also, you usually find that you get more information from a computer spreadsheet than from paper work. The reason for this lies in the use of formulas in the computer version. A change made in one cell gives immediate answers in many other cells.

QUESTIONS

1. In screen cell C5 you see 24. That could be because file cell C5 contains the number 24. What are two other things that could be in the file cell?

2. A file cell contains the formula +B5+B6+B7+B8. If you use a function, what formula will give the same result?

3. Suppose the numbers 8, 3, and 4 are visible in screen cells F1, G5, and H3. File cell M9 contains the formula @AVG(F1,G5,H3). What will appear in screen cell M9?

4. How do you write a range of cells? Give an example of a range of cells in the same column.

5. What character separates items in a cell list? Give an example of a list that contains one cell name and two ranges.

6. Suppose file cell D3 contains the value 63. File cell D4 contains the label 7. File cell D5 is blank. What value is returned by the function @SUM(D3..D5)?

7. File cell Q38 contains the formula 2*P38+Q37. What sentence tells the meaning of this formula? Use the words "left," "right," "above," and "below" in the sentence instead of the actual cell names.

8. You want to put a formula in file cell W73. The formula should calculate the average of the numbers in the cells to the left and to the right of cell W73. What is the formula?

9. File cell M42 contains the formula 5+M41. You copy this formula into file cells C10 and C11. When asked, you pick the relative mode of copying cell name M41. What formula will be in file cells C10 and C11?

10. File cell H5 contains a formula for multiplying the numbers in the first two cells to the left of H5. What is the formula?

11. You decide to move a copy of the formula in question 10 to file cell K13. You want the new formula to multiply the two numbers just left of the new cell K13. What copy mode should you use? What formula will be in file cell K13 if you use that mode?

12. Suppose you want to add a new row to the middle of a spreadsheet file. Where should you put the cursor? What command should you give?

13. If you add a new column to a spreadsheet file, what happens to the cell names in formulas?

14. What makes spreadsheet programs useful for answering what-if questions about numerical data?

Part D.

▪ Keyboard Commands

[⌘ B], **Blank** Blank out one or more spreadsheet cells. After blanking, a file cell contains neither a label nor a value. The screen cell is blank.

[⌘ C], **Copy** Duplicate a row, column, or block of cells at a new place in the spreadsheet file.

[⌘ D], **Delete** Delete one or more columns or rows. After deletion, cell names in formulas are changed relatively.

[⌘ I], **Insert** Insert one or more columns or rows. After insertion, cell names in formulas are changed relatively.

[⌘ N], **Name** Change the name of a file.

[⌘ P], **Print** Create a file copy on paper.

[⌘ Y], **Yank** When entering information into a file cell, erase characters from the cursor to the end of the line.

[⌘ Z], **Zoom** Switch the screen display from the usual screen cells to the file cells. This is useful for seeing which file cells contain formulas.

▪ New Ideas

cell cursor A bright rectangle that highlights a cell on a spreadsheet. To move through a spreadsheet file, you use keyboard commands to move the cell cursor.

cell indicator An area at the lower left corner of the screen that shows the location of the cell cursor, the type of information stored in that file cell, and the information itself. This is important when the information is a formula. The cell indicator always shows what the file cell contains.

cell name A letter followed by a number. The letter specifies a column in the spreadsheet; the number specifies a row.

file cell Part of a spreadsheet file. Information in a file cell tells the computer what to display in the corresponding screen cell. Formulas are in file cells; the results of the formulas appear in the corresponding screen cells. The cell indicator always shows what the file cell contains.

first-key rule A rule the computer follows when determining if a cell is to contain a value or a label. The first key tapped determines if a value or a label follows.

formula An expression in a file cell; it tells how to calculate a value to be displayed in the same screen cell.

function A built-in set of instructions for calculating values. Function names begin with the symbol @ and can be used in formulas.

label A type of information that can be entered into a spreadsheet file. An example is a string of characters used to describe the numbers on the spreadsheet.

no-change mode An instruction telling the computer how to treat a copied formula. When copying a formula containing a cell name, the computer makes no change in the cell name in the copy.

relative mode An instruction telling the computer how to treat a copied formula. When copying a formula containing a cell name, the computer changes the cell name in the copy in such a way that the meaning of the formula remains the same.

screen cell A cell on the screen that displays the results of the instructions contained in the same file cell.

spreadsheet size Up to 999 rows and 127 columns. The actual size of the spreadsheet is limited by the memory available.

value A type of information that can be entered into a spreadsheet file. Examples are numbers and formulas.

Index